ACKNOWLEDGEMENTS

Special thanks to:
Jerry Schmitz
Eric Doney
Russell Oakes

Thanks also to:
Todd Hensley and C&T Publishing who believed in giving credit where credit is due and went the extra mile for the quilters.

Sharon Pilcher whose persistence, support, friendship and caring contributed immeasurably to this book.

The families and loved ones of each of the stunt quilters who have learned to ask, "What does she want this time?" when I telephone.

Denise, Dennis and Emily Brent, Keith Yocam, Ron and Lucy Winters, Debbie Fetch and Kathy Allsman who kept hearth and home together during the insane times and never let me get too full of myself.

Scott, Richard, Laura and all those at C'est Si Bon who fueled my energy level.

Clark and Theresa Carmen (my satellite office staff) at Mailboxes Newport who copied, fax'ed, mailed and shipped with speed and efficiency.

The cast and crew of *How to Make an American Quilt*, especially Midge Sanford, Sarah Pillsbury, Mia Levinson, Jocelyn Moorhouse and Amie McCarthy who let me live out a real life fairy tale and always made me feel a part of the movie magic.

Additional thanks to the following individuals who participated in this project:

Stephen Anastas
Richard Ax
Dana Crackower
Steve Dontanville
Sarah L. Douglas
Michael Dunning
Kira Endsley
Meredith S. Fine
Karen Friedman
Stuart Fry
Toni Howard
Kevin Huvane
Georgia LaForce

Danny Mermel
Renee Milliken
Irene Navarro
Flora Roberts
Doug Robinson
Jeffrey Roda
Dave Rodgers
Margaret Rolfe
Nancy Safran
Todd Smith
Susan Smith
Perry Zimel

DEDICATION

Dedicated to Whitney Otto and her original vision; my mother, Barbara, a friend and role model, who nurtured an appreciation of the arts in me; my father, Bill, who taught me I could accomplish anything I put my mind to; my husband, Bill, who allowed me the opportunity to do this and has patiently waited for life to get back to normal; my sister, Susan, who loves me no matter what I do; and to my family of quilt friends who motivate and encourage me to constantly strive for something more. It's been an E ticket ride!

CONTENTS

INTRODUCTION

I wrote a novel called *How to Make an American Quilt*™, and it became a movie called *How to Make an American Quilt*.

I don't quilt. To paraphrase one of the story's characters, the women in my family don't quilt either. People are often surprised to learn that I am not a quilter. I explain that I am a writer—a fiction writer—which means I often depict worlds imagined within my own head: the town of Grasse, for example, is wholly fictitious, as are its citizens. I make things up.

It is said that fiction is the lie that tells the truth. So I am very flattered when readers assume I quilt, or that I have a grandmother and great-aunt who await my visits to their rambling old house. In a curious turn of thought, people seem to expect that fiction writers do not write fiction at all; that, in fact, novels are really just thinly veiled autobiographies. I think this confusion arises from that often misunderstood phrase "write what you know."

Along with my imaginary quilters came a handful of imaginary quilts. No one cared if the quilts actually existed, or about the specifics of their appearance. It simply did not matter—until they had to be seen in a movie. And there was no use asking me to design or draw a picture of the various quilts (recall that I am not a quilter), and that is how I ended up meeting Patty McCormick.

Amblin (Steven Spielberg's production company) contacted Patty, asking her to be the Technical Advisor for the movie.

Then, one day . . . there you are, running your hands across a quilt that previously existed on the edge of your own dream.

However, she ended up being a sort of Quilt Everyman: she gathered together the group of women who became known as the Stunt Quilters; she helped sew the quilts; she taught quilting classes for the actors (developing a particularly close and fruitful quilting friendship with Anne Bancroft, one of the women who had quilted before being cast in the movie); she acted as an extra, a hand double, a foot double. She made a special quilt for the director, Jocelyn Moorhouse. Patty was on the set every day, all day, cheerful and, I think, proud of the work she was doing. And she did wonderful work.

The first time I visited the set I was introduced to Patty, who offered to show me *Where Love Resides*® (Finn's wedding quilt). This particular day the quilt was hanging in a large, nearly empty room. When I saw it I was quite overcome. It was nothing like I had imagined, and more beautiful and perfect than I would have thought. "Look," said Patty, showing me the reverse side. And there, in the upper corner, it said this quilt was made in honor of Finn and Sam's wedding, followed by the names of each character.

My characters made this quilt, I thought. The stunt quilters did such fine work it was difficult for me to believe my characters actually didn't make this quilt. Patty gave me a sort of "tour" of the quilt: explaining, showing, telling stories—while I tried to compose myself, not wanting anyone to see my eyes beginning to tear, or hear my voice as it caught.

A writer lives in her head; her characters and locations are essentially abstract, always out of reach. I mean, you can't really touch or hold anyone or anything that lives on the page. Then, one day, some people say they are making a movie about those same characters and locations and, well, there you are, running your hands across a quilt that previously existed on the edge of your own dream.

I did not design *Where Love Resides*, I only left clues lying around my book. It took someone like Patty, and the other quilters, to translate my images, to pull this quilt from a story written by a non-quilter. For that, I thank them.

Whitney Otto
author of *How to Make an American Quilt*

Author Whitney Otto, left, and Patty McCormick standing in front of *Where Love Resides*.

The question I am asked most frequently is, "How did you get the job of Technical Advisor for a major motion picture?" I've thought of lots of reasons, but it all comes down to this: "Because I love quilters." I love the dynamics of quilting groups and the enthusiasm we share for even the most meager attempts. What other group celebrates what we call our "dog quilts" or revels in finding the perfect "ugly fabric" or justifies those big gloppy stitches by referring to them as "folky"? As a group of mostly women, we are working to change our image of "little old ladies" and of the old-fashioned quilting bee, and we are striving to gain acceptance and credibility in the art world.

When we expected to see a decline in the interest in quilting, it continued to grow. Quilt shows are attended by thousands every year—not just national shows, but small guild-sponsored shows. Our foremothers would be amazed to learn that quilts, which were originally meant to be used as nothing more than blankets, have attained such status. Quilts are being given as gifts to visiting foreign dignitaries, commissioned to hang on corporate office walls, and shown at organized exhibits in major museums and galleries around the world. For these reasons and so many others, I have actively participated in quilting since 1981, when I took my first quilting class at a local quilt shop.

I am one of the founding members of my guild, Flying Geese Quilters, located in Irvine, California. I am also currently President of the Southern California Council of Quilt Guilds, which is how I actually got to work as Technical Advisor on *How to Make an American Quilt.*

On August 24, 1994, I received a phone call on my message machine at home while I was (where else?) at a quilt show. The caller didn't identify herself other than to say she was working with a group of people who wanted to make a movie about quilts, and they were looking for someone to help them. As President of the Council, I frequently get requests from people who are looking for someone in their area to help them start or finish a project.

. . . I received a phone call on my message machine at home while I was (where else?) at a quilt show.

When I picked up the message, I was tired and considered putting off returning the phone call until another time, but the voice on the message sounded young (I guessed it was a Girl Scout troop working on a badge) and a little desperate, so I called her back.

During my phone call it was unclear to me what this was all about—not that this person was being vague, but she really didn't know anything about quilts or much about this "project"; her job was just to find someone who could help them.

Before I could direct her to the appropriate resource, I felt I needed more information about what the group was trying to accomplish, so we agreed to meet. She said she would get her group together and we would meet in Universal City (the first hint, but I didn't catch on) in Los Angeles. She also said she would send me a copy of the script overnight (a second hint, but I still didn't have a clue).

After I hung up, my husband Bill asked what the phone call was all about. I told him about the conversation and how confusing it was, but that I was going to meet with some people in Universal City and get more information. Now, I am not all that familiar with Los Angeles, so I asked him if Universal City was anywhere near Studio City or Universal Studios. He told me Universal City was Universal Studios. My confusion was growing and his interest was piqued. He asked if I knew whom I was talking to and I told him her name was Michelle, and that she worked with a group called "Ambling" or "Amble" or something like that. I really wasn't sure.

Patty and her friends at the quilt show.

At this point he looked at me like I had just walked out of the Stone Age and said, "Was it Amblin? Do you know what that is?" Now ask me to identify antique quilt blocks or recall a guest lecturer from ten years ago and I'll give you an instant answer. Ask me who directed or produced a movie I saw two weeks ago and I couldn't tell you, so I had no idea what Amblin was. My husband was incredulous that I didn't know this and he said, "It's Steven Spielberg's company!" I looked right at him and said, "No way. What's he doing making a movie about quilts?" Now I was really confused.

As promised, the script arrived the next morning by overnight delivery and I was even more surprised! The title of the project was *How to Make an American Quilt*. Back in 1991 when the book, written by Whitney Otto, was first published I got several copies from friends and family members who thought it was the perfect gift for me. And I liked the book. I immediately read the script, but it was different from how I remembered the book. I then reread the book in preparation for the meeting I was having with this unknown group.

I live in Orange County, California. Not really the sticks, but not the big city, either. And I'm a quilter. My wardrobe reflects both of those influences and I'm "taking a meeting" in Hollywood. Of course, I had to buy a new outfit. Something sort of Hollywood chic, and it had to be black (even though it's midday in August) that didn't scream "cutesy" and "quilter" from a mile away. I tell you this because, when I walked into the meeting, it was like a real-life advertisement for The Gap®. I was overdressed by about 1000 percent. It was the first of many lessons I would learn about the business.

At this meeting were the producers, co-producer, director, costume designer, production designer, several artists from the art department, the prop master, and several assistants. And Michelle had been right: they knew practically nothing about quilts. From the very beginning, everyone involved wanted to be sure the movie would be true to quilts, quilters, and quilting. They were three weeks into pre-production, had virtually nothing but the script and lots of ideas, and realized they needed a quilter right away. My initial intent was to teach them a little about quilts as they related to the script (I had taken lots of my own quilts, quilt tops, and blocks), find out what they needed, and then direct them to someone in the Los Angeles area who could help them. Halfway through the meeting, I realized I was having a lot of fun and that I could do this job.

Originally, all they wanted was a consultant, someone they could call on when they had a question or problem. They quickly realized the job was going to be much more involved.

◆

Halfway through the meeting, I realized I was having a lot of fun and that I could do this job.

At the first meeting the production designer, Leslie Dilley, showed me what he had so far. (I did not realize at the time that Les had won Academy Awards for art direction for *Star Wars* and *Raiders of the Lost Ark*.) He showed me a large piece of paper with a "quilt" drawn on it—empty blocks, four by six. I pointed out to him that there were seven women in the friendship group and, according to the story, each one makes a block for the quilt. Where were they planning to get the other seventeen blocks? I give the art department a lot of credit: they were five men who had probably never sewn a button on before, much less made a quilt, but they were wonderful to work with and soon accepted the fact I knew what I was talking about.

My job was now threefold: work in pre-production with the art and wardrobe departments in designing or acquiring the quilts, teach the actors in the friendship group how at least to look like they were sewing or quilting, and be on the set whenever a sewing scene was filmed to make sure things were accurate and authentic. I also lent several antique quilts from my own and a friend's collections to the set designer. The quilts were considered props, so I was primarily accountable to the props department. (I learned that "props" are items which are touched by actors, and that everything else is part of set decoration.)

I asked a number of my friends to participate, and they jumped at the chance. . . . Soon, we were referred to as the stunt quilters.

The original script called for five quilts, but gave very little description of what they were to look like. Although one or two of them could have been purchased, I opted instead to put together a team of quilters and make all five quilts. I had about two and a half months to make everything we needed. In "Hollywood time," that's more than adequate (they are used to having things done immediately); in "quilt time," it was a miracle we met all of the deadlines. I asked a number of my friends to participate, and they jumped at the chance. I was introduced to four new quilters who quickly became friends. In all, I had twelve quilters working on the quilts. They were invaluable in completing the project. Soon, we were referred to as the stunt quilters.

Three of the stunt quilters, from left to right: Linda Sawrey, Arnette Jasperson, and Jane Coscarelli.

Dr. Maya Angelou
Anna

Anne Bancroft
Glady Joe

Ellen Burstyn
Hy

Kate Nelligan
Constance

Jean Simmons
Em

Lois Smith
Sophia

Alfre Woodard
Marianna

The Grasse Quilting Bee Quilt

Jan Barbieri
Cordie Gary

Marianna's Baby Quilt

Jane Coscarelli
Cordie Gary
Patty McCormick
Linda Sawrey

Where Love Resides

Linda Aiken
Barbara Brown
Jane Coscarelli
Christine Dabbs
Kelly Gallagher-Abbott
Michelle Hilsabeck
Arnette Jasperson
Patty McCormick
Bobbie-Frances McDonald
Linda Sawrey

The Crazy Quilt

Christine Dabbs

The Life Before

Barbara Brown
Dora Simmons

Where Love Resides (108" x 108")

The Grasse Quilting Bee makes this quilt
during the course of the movie. It was
always going to be a friendship quilt.

WHERE LOVE RESIDES

The Grasse Quilting Bee gathers together, during the course of the movie, to make this quilt in honor of Finn's wedding. It was always going to be a friendship quilt. One of the original design ideas was to put the friendship blocks inside Double Wedding Rings. However, when we designed it, the rings had to be so large in order to hold the friendship blocks that the quilt was twice king-size and looked very odd. That idea was scrapped immediately.

The art department then went to resource books and studied antique quilts, especially friendship quilts. They came up with a Baltimore Album-style quilt based on an actual quilt from 1873. The design for the alternate blocks of blue vases and red flowers was inspired by that quilt; the border design was inspired by another antique quilt dated 1848. The friendship blocks came from the story: each block represents a significant part of the quilter's life.

The most important aspect of this quilt was that it is a friendship quilt, made by a group of women, some of whom had been together for over thirty-five years. They had shared life's experiences, both good and bad, and had moved in and out of the group,

The stunt quilters working on *Where Love Resides*. Left to right: Jane Coscarelli, Linda Sawrey, Arnette Jasperson, Patty McCormick

The Grasse Quilting Bee working on their quilting techniques. Left to right: Dr. Maya Angelou, Jean Simmons, Lois Smith, Anne Bancroft, Kate Nelligan, Ellen Burstyn

but always looked at the group as an anchor in their lives. This is a lot like my friendship group (except for the thirty-five years), so that's where I started looking for the quilters to create this quilt. Four of my friends immediately jumped at the opportunity to help me make the quilt. The quilt had a crazy-patch heart, and I knew one crazy quilter. Another friend from my guild offered to help, so that took care of the seven friendship blocks. The quilt also has eight alternate blocks, and then there's that border! The border alone has over 650 leaves on it.

Gladioli and Hyacinths from *Where Love Resides*. Designed by Linda Aiken.

I had taken a workshop from Laurene Sinema and she mentioned an appliqué group that met regularly at her shop, The Quilted Apple, in Phoenix, Arizona. I went to Phoenix to meet with Laurene to see if this group would make the border and alternate blocks for this quilt. Oh, did I mention we needed two complete tops (one would be quilted and bound, and one would remain a top) and seven sets of blocks? The extra sets of blocks were made in various stages of "in progress" so they could be used throughout the shooting of the movie. I went to her shop and rolled out a full-size pattern of the quilt. I started to pitch my idea to Laurene when she said, "I have just the person for you." I started to explain how much work was involved and the very tight deadlines we had to meet, and she assured me this person was perfect for the job. She made a phone call and I overheard her saying, "Universal Studios...Steven Spielberg...movie quilt...chance of a lifetime." Within ten minutes Linda Aiken walked into the shop. Two months later she gave me two complete borders (that's over 1300 hand appliquéd leaves, 100 little red flowers with reverse appliqué centers and lots of little rosebuds), 3 sets of alternate blocks (that is 24 exactly the same, all hand appliquéd) and 3 additional blocks. After we put the top together, I mailed it back to Linda overnight so she could finish appliquéing the borders around the corners.

If you have seen the movie and you do the math, you'll see the number of quilters doesn't add up to the number of friendship blocks. There are seven members of the Grasse Quilting Bee, but eight friendship blocks in the quilt. Linda became the character for the eighth friendship block and designed the basket of gladioli and hyacinths. This is a tribute to the two sisters in the story, Glady Joe and Hy, and also adds a little bit of quilters' humor.

This is a tribute to the two sisters in the story, Glady Joe and Hy . . .

Anne Bancroft, left, as Glady Joe and Ellen Burstyn as Hy working on *Where Love Resides*.

The Alternate block from *Where Love Resides*. Made by Linda Aiken.

Border made by Linda Aiken.

While I was at the Quilted Apple, Linda, Linda's friend named Nancy, Laurene, and I pulled the fabric for the alternate blocks and border. The friendship blocks were so different from each other that I knew it was the alternate blocks that would pull the whole quilt together. There was no rhyme or reason as to how we pulled the fabrics or which fabrics we chose; we just put together a palette we liked. I left that afternoon with little swatches of each of the fabrics we had chosen so I could go home and pull matching fabrics for the remaining blocks.

The House block is made by Glady Joe, the character played by Anne Bancroft. It was to be a replication of the house where she lived in Grasse. Despite our best efforts, the first drawing I received from the studio was impossible to put together. A friend from my guild, Bobbie-Frances McDonald, chose to make this block. However, she wasn't sure she wanted to do it after she saw the first design. We were told to make the house gray, but a mock-up of the block looked like a prison. The art department had drawn a couple sitting in a swing on the porch, but the people were two stories tall and totally out of proportion to the house. On both sides of the house the artists had drawn trees that were chopped in half where the block ended and they wanted the background to be blue sky. It was *not* what we envisioned.

The house where Glady Joe and Hy lived was a challenge for Bobbie-Frances to design.

The House block from *Where Love Resides* designed by Bobbie-Frances McDonald.

Bobbie-Frances asked for pictures of the actual house (which is in Santa Paula, California) and completely redesigned the block. She made it look more like the real house, including the weathervane on the roof. The redesigned block looked much better. She used pieces of gradated silk moiré ribbon for the windows and antique lace from her own collection for the railings and widow's walk. She didn't have black lace, so she carefully colored a cream-colored piece of antique lace with an indelible black fabric marker. Each friendship block in the quilt contains a significant piece of fabric from the character's life. In this block the roof is made from a piece of Glady Joe's husband's tie.

Each friendship block . . . contains a significant piece of fabric from the character's life.

Bobbie-Frances McDonald working in her studio.

The Mermaid block from *Where Love Resides* made by Jane Coscarelli.

The Mermaid block is made by the character Sophia, played by Lois Smith. Jane Coscarelli, a quilter from Murietta, California, actually made the block. The significant fabric in this block is the light blue print from the dress Sophia is wearing when she goes for a swim in the rock quarry. I doubt we had more than a quarter of a yard of this fabric and Jane had to make nine blocks. In the original design the light blue fabric was all that was to be used for the seaweed, but we realized we wouldn't be able to do that. Not only did we not have enough fabric to make all nine blocks, there wasn't enough contrast between that fabric and the background to see the shape of the seaweed. At one point I even tried photocopying a piece of the fabric onto muslin: it transferred, but was not a workable alternative, especially for turning under the appliqué. Instead, Jane appliquéd dark fabric underneath the lighter print. This not only allowed the dress fabric to pop out, but gave the block some depth.

Lois Smith as Sophia at work on the Mermaid block.

The Artist's Palette block from *Where Love Resides* made by Arnette Jasperson.

Now, remember those five non-sewing men from the art department who thought they could design quilts? They gave this mermaid an exposed breast. I don't know about you, but if I'm making a friendship block depicting myself that is to go into a Baltimore Album-style quilt to be given as a wedding gift, I don't think I would make myself half naked. There was some discussion about this and we finally just decided to make her hair longer, thereby covering any exposure. I like to think this is why the movie got a PG-13 rating.

The artist's palette is a block made by the character Em, played by Jean Simmons. Arnette Jasperson, another quilter from Murietta, California, made this block. Though simple in design, it was not as easy to make as it looks. The palette had to be made from a patterned heavy green velvet. The velvet is the significant fabric in this block: it comes from drapes that hang behind the couches in Em's husband's art studio. I saw the movie three times before I spotted the drapes. If you look closely, you'll see little bits of this green velvet in several of the blocks. I figured this group had to be like my friendship group and shared fabric. Even though, as Whitney Otto describes them, they are not warm, huggy women, they do have this undeniable friendship—a bond I tried to bring out in the quilt.

The next friendship block is made by Anna, the character Dr. Maya Angelou portrays. I made this block using the pattern Barbara Brown had designed for the Marriage block in *The Life Before* quilt. Anna owns the family heirloom quilt given to her by her Aunt Pauline, which tells the story of her family and how her grandparents met. The block in

Anne Bancroft, left, as Glady Joe and Dr. Maya Angelou as Anna.

this quilt is a duplication of the Marriage block in *The Life Before* quilt. The love relationship in Anna's life is with her daughter and she passes on her family story to Finn. The significance of the crow becomes evident near the end of the movie. The sun design was added to update the block and is a Mariner's Compass. The woman's dress is made from authentic fabric from the Ivory Coast in Africa, and the significant fabric in this block is the man's shirt. The only person I have talked to who identified the significant fabric as being the shirt is the fifteen-year-old daughter of a friend. Margie said she recognized it immediately as a piece of the dress Anna was wearing when she went into labor with her daughter, Marianna. Since the love of her life is really her daughter, it had to be that dress.

The laurel wreath with the two gold wedding rings is Hy's block. Hy was played in the movie by Ellen Burstyn. Originally, the design was two big rings: an engagement ring with a huge diamond, and a wedding band. The production team initially wanted the rings to be silver. We made one block and, once again, it was *not* what we had envisioned. Hy didn't wear a diamond ring, the rings were totally out of proportion to the rest of the quilt, and the silver gray was flat. Several of the stunt quilters were at the Pacific International Quilt Festival in Northern California in October when we decided to redesign this block. The laurel wreath was more in keeping with the feel of the quilt. We knew we couldn't talk the studio out of using the rings, but we could make them smaller. Jane Coscarelli designed the block and Michelle Hilsabeck, a quilter from Wildomar, California, made the blocks.

The Marriage block designed by Barbara Brown.

Originally, the design was two big rings: an engagement ring with a huge diamond, and a wedding band.

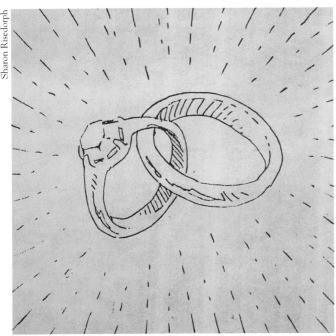

Sharon Risedorph

The original Ring block as designed by the art department.

The redesigned Ring block designed by Jane Coscarelli and made by Michelle Hilsabeck.

The gold lamé in this block was certainly not our idea. While we were in Northern California, I invited the prop master to come to the quilt show to shop for sewing supplies and props for the movie. We had a wide selection of vendors and we could get it all done at one time. Imagine how much fun it was to spend someone else's money and buy all new supplies. I learned that when you need one, you buy six just to be safe. But during that wild shopping spree, the prop master saw the gold lamé in Katie Pasquini Masopust's booth. Remember, the quilts were considered props, so he had some influence and insisted we use the gold lamé for the rings. Although I didn't think gold lamé had a place in the quilt, we had already used silk moiré ribbon, green and red velvet, pink satin, and yellow 100% polyester. Why not a little gold lamé? The first time I saw the quilt laid out on the floor in the movie, it was so beautifully lit that the rings just shimmered. I have to admit, I like the gold lamé.

The crazy-patch heart belongs to Marianna, played by Alfre Woodard, because she had a crazy-patch love life with several different men. Her one true soul mate was a man she met in Paris, which explains the importance of

Alfre Woodard as Marianna with the purse that inspired the Heart block.

The significant fabric is . . . part of a purse she is carrying when she meets this man in Paris.

The Crazy-Patch Heart block from *Where Love Resides* made by Christine Dabbs.

the Eiffel Tower in the block. The significant fabric is the piece of crazy patch which is part of a purse she is carrying when she meets this man in Paris. Unfortunately you never really see the purse in the scene. Marianna is not really into quilting, but she belongs to the group because she moved back to Grasse and her mother belongs to the group. This was the perfect style of block not only for Marianna, but also for the actor. The first time I met Alfre, she said to me, "Good luck, I have hands of stone." This block was made by Christine Dabbs (who doesn't have hands of stone).

The last friendship block on the quilt is Chickie's Garden, made by Constance, the character played by Kate Nelligan. This block was actually made by Linda Sawrey, my best friend. Linda and I took our first quilting class together fourteen years ago. She lives in Temecula, California, and is a member of the Valley of the Mist

Kate Nelligan as Constance sitting in the yellow rose garden that inspired her block Chickie's Garden.

Quilters. To me, this block is the most important block in the quilt and carries a strong quilt story which didn't get picked up in the movie. It is representative of the rose garden Constance's husband planted and in which their dog, Chickie, is buried. It is a yellow rose garden and she makes the flowers out of one of her husband's old shirts (this is the yellow 100% polyester fabric nightmare).

Constance was recently widowed, so this block holds more meaning for her than some of the other blocks do to the other characters. She is not willing to compromise her block, but the other quilters all hate the yellow fabric. As Anna says, "It throws the whole damn balance off!" Rather than change her block or defend herself (there is a subplot in the film about Constance having an affair with a one of the other quilter's husbands), she chooses to take her block and leave the group. Yet several scenes later she's back at the quilting frame with the rest of the group. Now how did that happen? I put how it happened in the quilt. Remember, this group has been together for a long time and lived through a lot of experiences together. It's not easy to give that up, and the group doesn't really want to lose Constance. To get her back, everyone compromises. They realize they have become an important part of each others' lives, so they are willing to put a piece of that ugly yellow fabric into each of their blocks—in essence, putting Constance into their stories. In turn, Constance takes a piece of orange from Glady Joe's orange tree, a piece of Sophia's dress (as if we really had any extra!), and the green velvet from Em's drapes and puts them into her block.

> ### To me, this is the most important block in the quilt and carries a strong quilt story . . .

Isn't that what friendship groups are? We are all a part of each others' stories. So the final quilt you see spread out on the floor is the first time you see the blocks with the yellow fabric in them. Up until then, when the quilters are working on their individual blocks or when the blocks are on the design wall, the mermaid has brown hair and there is no sun in Anna's block. The yellow fabric isn't seen anywhere except in Chickie's Garden.

Chickie's Garden block from *Where Love Resides* made by Linda Sawrey.

When all the blocks were completed, we put the two tops together. I realized I had a lot going on in the middle of this quilt and had a very ornate border. I chose the two inner borders to control and separate the outer border from the center of the quilt (sounds like an underwire bra) and was pleased with the final result. It took Linda Sawrey and me about twelve hours to lay out and piece that first top.

Here's another movie secret: there is some machine quilting on this quilt. Arnette Jasperson, who made the Artist's Palette block,

Linda Sawrey at work attaching the inner border with her cat Simba.

Here's another movie secret: there is some machine quilting on this quilt.

Arnette Jasperson machine quilting in the ditch around the blocks and border.

machine quilted in the ditch around the blocks and borders and around the vine in the outer border. Linda Sawrey, Jane Coscarelli, Arnette Jasperson, Michelle Hilsabeck and I then hand quilted the entire surface of this king-size quilt in 2″ crosshatching. The hand quilting took eight days—in hoops, not in a frame. The quilt had to be very portable. Where the quilt went depended on who was off work, who didn't have kids, or who had called in sick. At least one person worked on the quilt eight to ten hours a day for each of those eight days. There was one evening we had five hoops on it. Amazingly, the quilt lays perfectly flat, and we met our deadline.

In Hollywood, the original script is never the final script; there are changes being made daily. So it didn't surprise me when the director wanted to add something after the quilt was finished. She wanted a scene where Finn, played by Winona Ryder, wakes up with the finished quilt over her and sees a label which reads "Presented to Finn and Sam on the occasion of their wedding." And, true to form, the director wanted it the next day. I realized this couldn't be just a simple label and knew there was only one friend I could call to help me. Kelly Gallagher-Abbott makes beautiful labels for her quilts and teaches label-making in workshops. I called her and explained what I needed. She told me she was having a dinner party that evening, but she would do as much as she could. She would leave the label in an envelope on her doorstep for me to pick up on my way to the studio at 5:30 the next morning with instructions on what I had to do if she didn't finish making it. I would then have to sew it onto the quilt in time. Kelly stayed up most of the night finishing the label, which she designed, hand painted, stitched, and lettered beautifully. It was exactly what they wanted and was perfect for the scene. All I had to do was sew it on. What? You don't remember seeing the label? Check the cutting-room floor. All that work and they decided not to use it.

A part of the movie I am always blamed for takes place near the end. Finn is running through the orange

Hand quilting *Where Love Resides*. Left to right: Jane Coscarelli, Arnette Jasperson, Patty McCormick

grove with the quilt wrapped around her and it's dragging on the ground. Let me set the record straight—it wasn't my fault! Every quilter I have spoken with brings up that scene. They tell me they heard a collective gasp in the theater as the audience watched this beautiful white quilt being dragged through the dirt. Few of them mentioned anything about

the next scene where the quilt is spread out in the back of a filthy, greasy Volkswagen bus. Well, I almost fainted watching that scene being shot. But the quilt was dirty before I could do anything about it. Winona is very petite and that quilt is 108″ long and heavy. It was wrapped around her as high as possible and it just dropped to the ground while she was running. I have rationalized the scene in my mind. What she was running towards was of the utmost importance to her; nothing else mattered at that moment—not even this brand new beautiful white quilt that her grandmother's friendship group had spent the last "72 hours" quilting. And that's what the story is all about—love. The love of a man, the love of your daughter, the love of your friends. It's not about how to make a quilt.

This quilt was given to Jane Anderson, the screen writer, who loves the fact that it is dirty; I refer to it as "Winonadirt." The unfinished quilt top used in the final quilting scene was finished after the movie was completed. It was given to Whitney Otto, the author of the novel on which the movie was based.

The label to record the making of *Where Love Resides* designed, hand painted, stitched, and lettered by Kelly Gallagher-Abbott.

(Patterns for this quilt are provided on pages 56–85.)

This quilt was to be a re-creation of an 1880s African-American story quilt made by slave ancestors of the character Anna. The art department struggled with this quilt. Their only reference was the Smithsonian Museum's Bible Quilt by Harriet Powers, and everything they designed looked just like that quilt. These five men in the art department who didn't sew or quilt were also not African-American. This quilt was just not coming together for them, and we didn't have a lot of time.

During this period of time, a friend of mine showed me an article from the San Francisco *Chronicle* about an African-American quilter from Maryland, Barbara Brown. She designed and created Afrocentric quilts, and sounded like just the person I needed. So I called information, got her business number, and called her. (It always amazes me that quilters are so accessible.) After I described the project to her, she was very interested and agreed to send me some block designs. Since we live so far apart we had to depend on the telephone and fax machine for communication.

Each of the blocks was a 15½-inch square, so Barbara devised a way to send them. After she designed the first five blocks, she photocopied each block in fourths and fax'ed the pages to me with instructions on how to put them back together. After I taped them back together, I copied them onto a single sheet of paper.

The studio loved the first designs, so I commissioned Barbara to design all fifteen blocks. As she designed the blocks, she photocopied them in fourths and fax'ed them to me in groups of four or five at a time. Scenes depicted in this quilt are part biblical and part slave stories. She used an *adinkra* symbol for good fortune on the side of the cradle. According to Barbara, adinkra means "saying good-bye" in Twi, the language of the Akan people of Ghana.

> *This quilt was to be a re-creation of an 1880s African-American story quilt . . .*

The cradle with the adinkra symbol from *The Life Before* quilt designed by Barbara Brown.

The Life Before (56″ x 88″)

The next step was getting Barbara's designs made into a quilt. I asked Dora Simmons, a member of the Afro-American Quilters of Los Angeles, and an appliqué expert, if she would be interested in completing the quilt. It was important to me to maintain the integrity of the quilt by having it designed and made by African-American quilters. The quilt had to look 110 years old, so I chose all Cherrywood solid, dyed fabrics on muslin backgrounds. Dora used some print fabric, when appropriate, from her own stash. She designed the set, and used a scrappy lattice to pull all the blocks together. Dora was then to quilt and bind it.

But, as things happen in Hollywood, they changed the shooting schedule and wanted the quilt five days early. We were already on a very tight deadline, so this was a major problem. Dora had just put the quilt in the frame and was starting to quilt it when they told me they needed the quilt the next day. Up until this time I had not seen the quilt, except for the block designs. I intentionally stayed away because I did not want to influence the way the quilt looked.

Dora Simmons, maker of *The Life Before* quilt, with Elainia.

Dora had just put the quilt in the frame when they told me they needed the quilt the next day.

One of the drivers from the studio picked up the quilt from Dora and brought it to the studio. When I opened it up, I almost fainted. The block that depicted the parting of the Red Sea was right in the middle of the quilt and the water was done in red fabric. I thought the water was supposed to be blue. Dora told me she had done some research and learned that the water looks red because red sand from the surrounding desert blows over the surface of the sea. It has become my favorite block.

But I still had a quilt that needed to be quilted so they could use it the next day. It so happened that, while this was going on, we were also shooting a scene of close-up quilting. Whenever we did close-up quilting shots, I had several of my quilting friends act as hand doubles for the actors. Since several quilters were present, we quilted on it for the rest of the day. We had a long day of shooting, so we were able to finish it.

The quilt still looked new, so I stopped at the grocery store on the way home and bought a container of brown Rit® dye. I had never dyed or tea-dyed fabric, but I decided to give it a try with the props department's guidance. I filled the tub of my washing machine with hot water and added the dye. I looked at the brown water and realized there was only one of these quilts in the world. If I messed it up, I would have to leave the country and could never quilt in this town again. I plunged the quilt into the washing machine and followed the directions on the container. I took the quilt out about every two minutes to make sure nothing was going wrong. As soon as it got to the right color, I threw it into a hot dryer because I wanted it to "pucker up." I was pleased with the results and took it to the studio the next morning.

The Red Sea block from *The Life Before* quilt designed by Barbara Brown.

If I messed it up, I would have to leave the country and could never quilt in this town again.

Patty's cat Woody inspecting *The Life Before* quilt.

Doug Fox, the prop master, promptly took the cup of chamomile tea I was holding and to my horror, threw it on the quilt—more aging! He then snipped threads and loosened pieces of appliqué to make it look more authentic. This was where our philosophies differed; whereas I thought a cherished family heirloom would have been kept in excellent condition, he wanted the audience to know this was an old quilt. I guess he was right, because on more than one occasion, I have been asked if *The Life Before* really is an old quilt.

The Grasse Quilting Bee Quilt (79¹/2″ x 92″)

THE GRASSE QUILTING BEE QUILT

This quilt was to be used in one of the opening scenes. They were going to pan slowly over the quilt and then fade or transition into actual aerial footage shot from a helicopter. I was given a topographical map and an aerial photograph of the area outside Bakersfield, where the mythical town of Grasse is located. This quilt was going to require a lot of continuity and could not be made by a group. My friend, Jan Barbieri, offered to take on the task of making it.

Jan and I spent days pulling just the right fabrics to make it look like a map and still maintain the feeling of a quilt. This was also supposed to be a circa-1978 quilt, so our fabric choices were somewhat limited. A quilter with a sharp eye noticed we used a current piece of fabric designed by Nancy Crow; however, it worked in the

Jan Barbieri with her quilting companions, Demetrius and Pokey, working on *The Grasse Quilting Bee Quilt.*

Jan and I spent days pulling just the right fabrics to make it look like a map and still maintain the feeling of a quilt.

Detail of Nancy Crow fabric found in the quilt.

quilt. A good portion of the bottom of the quilt is orange groves and we were not able to find an appropriate representational fabric. It was a very important part of the quilt because this would be where the fade-out of the quilt and fade-in of the helicopter shot would take place. Our solution was for Cordie Gary, a quilter/artist/friend, to use photographs of the orange groves, to hand paint the actual shapes and configurations of the groves onto printed fabric. Using two different shades of green fabric paint, she was able to add depth to the fabric that we might not otherwise have been able to achieve. Jan worked tirelessly on this quilt, even taking parts of it on a trip to South Africa to visit family. In the movie the quilt is seen in a frame, so it did not have to be quilted or bound.

Three days before we were to shoot this scene, the cinematographer went up in the helicopter late in the afternoon to shoot the aerial footage. The orange groves where the transition was to take place from quilt to film were almost completely in shadow. The photographs we worked from were taken three months earlier (late November, early December) and didn't have the shadows. The orange groves on the film didn't look anything like the groves on the quilt. The cinematographer did not want to reshoot the scene, so he asked me if we could change the quilt. This was late on a Friday afternoon, and they had made arrangements for special cameras and cameramen to shoot the scene with the quilt on Monday morning. We had two and a half days to change the quilt and make the scene work.

The hand painted orange groves.

Our solution was . . . to use photographs of the orange groves, to hand paint the . . . groves . . .

I met with Jan early Saturday and we started evaluating different options. What finally worked (and has been a secret up until now) was to use a green Mary Ellen Hopkins fabric, cut into long squiggly rows and then fused to a 9″ by 24″ length of navy blue fabric. We didn't have time for any finished appliqué work. Jan then took a yellow grease pencil and drew in very fine lines between the trees that looked like the last glint of afternoon sun. We appliquéd this strip of fabric loosely to the corner of the quilt in the diagonal direction the camera would follow.

On Monday we laid the quilt out flat on a large table on the set. We scrunched the rows of orange groves to give them a more three-dimensional look. The nurseryman, in charge of all things green or growing, then stapled small leafy twigs all along the edge of the table. When they positioned the lights through the twigs the shadows made the orange groves look almost real. They used a remote-operated camera to line up the film footage with the quilt. It took ten hours to get it perfect. When I saw the movie for the first time, this scene took my breath away.

An aerial picture of the actual orange groves. Photo courtesy of Patty McCormick.

After they shot that scene I had this very beautiful quilt with this very ugly navy blue scar-like piece of fabric. They wanted to use the quilt in a second scene and were going to shoot from underneath the quilt so you could see hands on top of the quilt. All you could see was this dark diagonal 9″ by 24″ "thing." Another secret unveiled for the first time: you may not have noticed, but for this scene, I took the shadowed orange groves off the quilt.

During the scene, the stunt quilters were used because it involved close-up hand quilting. In order to shoot looking up from underneath the quilt, the props department had balanced the frame on two narrow runways about twelve feet off the floor. It was difficult to concentrate with glaring lights, wobbling chairs, and six cameramen filming from below.

Patty McCormick stitching on the shadows of the orange groves.

When we sat down to quilt, we all did what we normally do: we put our left hands underneath the quilt and started quilting with our right hands. The next thing we heard was, "Cut!" This is not what they wanted. They wanted to see a lot of hand activity on top of the quilt. I tried to explain that wasn't the way we quilted, but I lost that argument to cinematographic license. So here is my interpretation as to what is going on in that scene (other than a lot of thread and scissors being thrown back and forth): we all got to the end of our thread and were tying off and hiding our knots at exactly the same time!

Louise Berkley, one of my dearest quilting friends, was at the studio that day working as a hand double. She helped me sew and then remove the shadowed orange groves from the quilt twice during the day.

Jan finished quilting *The Grasse Quilting Bee Quilt* and it was given to Leslie Dilley, the production designer. It was his idea to use the quilt in the opening scene with the aerial shot.

The Zebra block from *Marianna's Baby Quilt* made by Linda Sawrey.

The direction I was given on this one was to make it ethnic . . .

The Monkey block from *Marianna's Baby Quilt* made by Cordie Gary.

nother quilt you never really see in the movie is the quilt the character young Anna, played by Maria Celedonio, is making during her pregnancy. The only part of the quilt you see is the Zebra block. The direction I was given on this one was to make it ethnic, dark, and not quite perfect. According to the script, it was made in the 1940s.

Pieced animals seemed to be the perfect choice for the blocks. I picked animals from Africa as the ethnic part, and pulled a lot of reproduction fabric from that era, as well as some authentic vintage fabric. Linda Sawrey made the Elephant and Zebra blocks, Jane Coscarelli made the Tiger and Rhinoceros blocks, and Cordie Gary made the Monkey and Camel blocks. Cordie also improved on the original set design by turning it sideways and framing each of the individual blocks before setting them in the pieced lattice.

Maria Celedonia as Young Anna and Claire Danes as Young Glady Jo.

The "not quite perfect" part of the quilt is that some of the framings are crooked and our math didn't always work out on the lattice strips. I added the two gold stars because of a line in the story where Anna wishes on a shooting star that her baby grows up to be like the sky, belonging to no one. The line was cut from the final film, but I liked the stars and kept them on the quilt.

Marianna's Baby Quilt (39″ x 36″)

Once the quilt was finished I showed it to my husband ("he who knows everything") and was explaining the significance of its different parts. He asked what African animal was in the upper middle block and I said it was a tiger. He informed me there are no tigers in Africa, they live in Asia, and without missing a beat I told him, "Oh, then it's a lioness." At the end of production this quilt was given to Alfre Woodard, because she has two small children.

(Patterns for this quilt are provided on pages 86–94.)

The Crazy Quilt (31¹/₂″ x 54″)

THE CRAZY QUILT

The original script called for a crazy quilt to be used in the opening scene. It was a "drag-around," unfinished crazy quilt that the character Finn played with as a child. The production team wanted two identical quilts, because they needed a back-up in case something happened to the first one. They intended to "age" the quilt to make it look like a child had dragged it around. The problem was, I didn't personally know anybody who was making crazy quilts. I then remembered seeing a crazy quilt the year before at the Orange County Fair. I had no idea who the maker was, so I had to track her down. No one knew her and she didn't belong to any of the local guilds, but after making several phone calls I was able to get her name and phone number.

That phone call began a friendship with Christine Dabbs. I can only imagine her initial response to my phone call. I was much more descriptive about identifying who I was and the project I was working on than when I had first been contacted. I explained I was working with Universal Studios and Steven Spielberg on a movie version of the book *How to Make an American Quilt*, that I needed two identical toddler-size crazy quilts, and that she would be paid for them. I told her the quilts would be "aged" by the prop department. I also explained the quilts didn't need to be very elaborate, because the scene was short. Only a portion of the quilt would be seen because it would be draped over the child, who would be peeking through a hole in it. We needed the quilts in about six weeks and, other than a few requests from the production team about what they wanted on the quilt, she could design it herself.

The original script called for a . . . "drag-around," unfinished crazy quilt that the character Finn played with as a child.

Young Finn, played by Kaelynn and Sara Craddick, sitting under the quilt frame with *The Crazy Quilt* in her lap.

I have since learned that Christine does not understand the instruction "not very elaborate." She made stunning quilts, exquisitely pieced from collected cottons, satins, silks, velvets, brocades, and ribbon, and stitched with intricate tiny stitches covering all of the seams. Christine embroidered the quilts entirely by hand (I don't think she even owns a sewing machine). She chose many motifs relating to the story, including an orange tree, a house, and a field of flowers, all in silk ribbon, and gladioli, and hyacinths (for the names of the two sisters in the story). She also included traditional motifs of peacock feathers, spiders and spider webs, and a fan. It took her more than 500 hours to make the two quilts.

Christine Dabbs and her cat Molly Ann.

She chose many motifs relating to the story, including an orange tree, a house, and a field of flowers...

Detail of orange tree from *The Crazy Quilt*.

She knew she was going to have to give the quilts up and that they would be aged, so she made a third quilt to keep for herself. Then she made two more, one for each of her daughters, and a sixth one just as an extra; then she made a seventh quilt as a gift for me. The last five quilts were stitched in silk thread and every seam was beaded, but they were otherwise identical to the movie quilts.

When I took her quilts to the studio and turned them over to the prop department, the prop master took one of them and went to work. He cut holes in it, sliced it, shredded it, and tore it. Then he painted the back of it brown with a stain that seeped through to the front so that it look older and dirty. Lastly, he put it in a large rotating tub with water and rocks to make it look really old. Ahhh, movie magic. What came out of that tub was a shadow of what had gone in, but it developed a patina of age that made it as wonderful as it was when it was new, but in a different way.

Detail of the house and flowers from *The Crazy Quilt*.

If you have seen the movie, I am sure you are asking yourself, "Where is the beautiful crazy quilt?"

Well, after all that work, the scene ended up on the cutting-room floor. If you watch very closely, you will briefly see the quilt in two scenes. When young Finn is sitting under the quilt frame, it's in her lap. Then you see the quilt again when, as an adult, Finn is packing to go to her grandmother's for the summer. She stuffed the quilt in a box to take with her. I loved the significance of this scene (though barely visible to the audience), that Finn's childhood quilt was still important to her as a young woman.

At the end of production, the studio gave the second quilt (which had not been aged) to Winona Ryder as a gift. Christine replaced the aged, working quilt with the extra quilt she had made and it was given to Midge Sanford, one of the producers. The aged, ripped, torn, stained, and washed crazy quilt seen in the movie is in Christine's collection.

. . .the prop master took one of. . .the quilts and cut holes in it, sliced it, shredded it, and tore it. Ahhh, movie magic.

THE FRIENDSHIP QUILT

$\mathcal{A}$ nother project I started about halfway through production was a friendship quilt. I had become very fond of everyone I was working with, and knew we would never be together again. I wanted to document this event, and what better way to do it than in a quilt. My plan from the beginning was to give the quilt to our director, Jocelyn Moorhouse, as a surprise. With the help of Mia Levinson, the producers' assistant who had access to a lot of the behind the scenes crew, and Eden Ashley, the film's publicist who worked closely with the actors, we started collecting signatures of the cast and crew. I chose a simple, 4¹/₂-inch Rail Fence block, and used a lot of the leftover fabric from the quilts, adding from my stash when needed. Blocks for the actor/quilters were made using a significant piece of fabric from their block on the quilt *Where Love Resides*. Kate Nelligan's block is made with that "damn ugly yellow fabric;" Lois Smith's block is made from a scrap of Sophia's dress; Jean Simmons's block is made from the green velvet. I constructed the blocks and ironed each one onto a piece of freezer paper for stability.

> *I had become very fond of everyone I was working with, and knew we would never be together again.*

We were able to get over 90 percent of the cast and crew to sign, partly because once the word got out, people were coming to me to sign blocks. I had everyone sign two blocks, telling them that if I made a mistake or lost one, I needed a back-up, all along knowing there would someday be two quilts and that I would keep one for myself. The only change on the second quilt is that I have included the signatures of all the stunt quilters without whom this whole project would not have been possible and who are integral to the "look" of this movie. In the quilters' blocks I used the same fabric I had used in the block for the actress they had done the quilting for. Linda Sawrey's block is also made out of that "damn ugly yellow fabric;" Jane Coscarelli's block is made from scraps of Sophia's dress; and Arnette Jasperson's block is made from the green velvet. We gave the quilt to Jocelyn at the wrap party after the filming ended. I was amazed to find out we had successfully pulled off the surprise. She didn't have a clue about the quilt.

Patty and director, Jocelyn Moorhouse, left, after receiving her *Friendship Quilt* at the post production party.

The Friendship Quilt (51″ x 70″)

Anne Bancroft as Glady Joe working on her House block.

THE ACTORS

*a*nother part of my job was to teach the actors how to quilt. I really didn't need to teach them how to quilt, but to just look as if they were quilting. They are not seen sewing or quilting that much in the movie, but they had to look convincing, because they had been sewing together for thirty-five years.

My goal was to get them to look comfortable with the different tools (like wearing thimbles, something they all had trouble with) and handling their quilt blocks. I met with each of the actors from The Grasse Quilting Bee (Dr. Maya Angelou, Anne Bancroft, Ellen Burstyn, Jean Simmons, Lois Smith, and Alfre Woodard) on an individual basis doing some one-on-one teaching. We then met several times as a group to quilt together.

Anne Bancroft had quilted before . . .
She caught on quickly.

Anne Bancroft had quilted before. During the making of the movie *84 Charing Cross Road* someone from the crew had taught her hand quilting, so she was not new to the techniques I was teaching. She caught on quickly. Her character was making the House block, so I concentrated on appliqué stitching with her.

Early in the filming schedule she came to me and asked if I had any fabric in a particular shade of rusty orange. She was wearing a long silk coat and had torn the corner of the front hem. She wanted to use her new appliqué skills and stitch a patch over the tear before it tore any more. At the studio I had set up quite a supply corner, practically moving my whole sewing room onto the set. I had to be prepared for just about any sewing necessity. If props didn't have it, I did. One of the things I had brought was a large box of scrap fabrics. Anne rummaged through the box and found just the perfect scrap, which she expertly appliquéd over the tear. Admiring her work, we both commented on how it sort of looked like an orange tree.

Detail of Anne Bancroft's coat that she appliquéd during breaks on the set. Photo courtesy of Patty McCormick.

Next thing I knew she had gone back to the scrap box and found just the perfect scrap of green. Now there was grass under the tree. Then there were clouds in the sky; then a moon; then a little house next to the tree, a chimney with smoke, and windows and a door. Next came a walkway. Then Josh from the art department had to design a car to put in the driveway and I'm stopping at the fabric store to find the perfect silver for the bumper.

This project took us through several long days of work, and sewing together made us friends. We would talk about our families (we're both the eldest of three girls and both our husbands have an affinity for wine collecting) and our plans for the holidays. Last time I saw the coat, she was planning the New York skyline to go along the back hem and considering a beach scene for the other front. By the end of the movie she told me she had bought a second coat with the intention of sewing houses on it.

During one of our afternoon sewing sessions, I asked about the quilt she made before. She told me she had never finished it, and that it was in a plastic bag on a closet shelf. She had developed tennis elbow while working on the quilt and thought the quilting had been the cause of her pain, so she put it away. She agreed to bring it to the studio so I could see it. It was wonderful, and almost finished! It was approximately twin-size, a white-on-white quilt. The quilting design was her front yard. It had palm trees and artichoke plants and lots of bushes and flowers, and the quilting template was still in the bottom of the bag. I watched her quilt in a hoop and couldn't figure out how she could possibly develop tennis elbow, when she admitted she was also playing a lot of tennis at that time. I offered to help. It seemed so appropriate for her to finish her project, while we were working on the movie *How to Make an American Quilt*.

I am a big proponent of giving unfinished projects life rather than letting them die in a plastic bag on a closet shelf. The first thing that needed to be done was to remark the part of the quilt that wasn't quilted. Having the original template made it easy and I quickly did this over a weekend. Then Anne quilted it. Remember, this is white-on-white and you

Kate Nelligan as Constance organizing her supplies.

cannot believe how dirty studios are, so she did a lot of the quilting in her trailer between scenes. When that was done, I sewed the binding on for her. She did a great job and proudly keeps the quilt (once destined for obscurity on the closet shelf) on her guest bed.

I never worked with Kate Nelligan, in part because, as Constance, she was not as much a part of the group as the others were, and she stayed in character on that point. You never see her working on her block in the movie; the only time she has a needle in her hand is at the end when they are all working at the quilt frame (and then we used hand doubles).

Dr. Maya Angelou had sewn as a child and was quick to pick up on piecing and quilting. As Anna, she is the "master quilter" of the group, so I mentally credit her with coming up with the idea for the quilt *Where Loves Resides*. In my mind, she is the one who made all the alternate blocks and that border.

Dr. Maya Angelou as Anna, the "master quilter" of the group.

In my mind, she is the one who made all the alternate blocks and that border.

We met the day before Thanksgiving for three hours in her hotel in Los Angeles. Once I showed her the fundamentals, she practiced and we did what any two women do when they get together to sew: we talked. She told me a childhood memory she had of her grandmother's general store. On Sunday afternoons the women who had been working all week long in the fields would come to the store and her grandmother would teach them fine hand sewing. She remembered the women's hands looking very rough and gnarled, yet they made beautiful, tiny stitches. It was a wonderful story. We then compared Thanksgiving menus and talked about how much work we both still had to do (she was having 120 people for dinner, I was having eight), and we talked a little about our families. It was a wonderful three hours that just flew by. She never reminded me that she was the Poet Laureate of the United States, and had read one of her poems at a Presidential inauguration. We were two women thrown together by circumstances, and I was showing her how to quilt.

Of all the actors, you see Ellen Burstyn sewing on her block, the Ring block, most often. She doesn't normally sew, but she got comfortable with needle and thread quickly. She works on a partially finished block that Michelle Hilsabeck had made and, if you watch closely, she keeps taking the same stitch over and over again. When we shot a scene we would do ten, twelve, maybe fifteen takes. From that group, the cinematographer and director would choose three or four, and then the editors chose the one scene that fit best into the movie. They would shoot the scene, which might be Ellen saying her line while stitching on her block. Before they reshoot the scene (take 2) I had to go in, take the stitches out of the block, put pins back where they were, and make sure the thread was about the same length so it looked exactly the same as before. When we did this ten or twelve times, I was threading a lot of needles.

Jean Simmons also doesn't sew, but she is the consummate actress. She worked very hard at making her stitching look perfect. In the scene where she gets angry and frustrated, she really is frustrated. For some

When we shot a scene we would do ten, twelve, maybe fifteen takes.

Ellen Burstyn as Hy at the sewing machine.

reason the green thread she was using kept breaking or knotting. Half the time she was sewing without thread in the needle. This was a good portion of the "hundreds of needles" I threaded during the course of the movie.

Lois Smith, who played Sophia, practiced her stitching technique religiously, wanting it to look perfect. When she wasn't filming she would come into the trailer they had given me while we were on location, for a little extra practice. She would take pieces and practice at night after work. In the movie Lois plays a character who in her middle years is always cranky and unhappy with her lot in life. However, in real life I found her delightful. Our sewing sessions allowed a lot of time for conversation.

Jean Simmons as Em worked very hard to make her stitching look perfect.

Alfre Woodard plays Marianna, who leads a Bohemian lifestyle until she returns to Grasse and settles down. Her block is the crazy-patch heart in the friendship quilt: not very orderly, not following the rules of design like the rest of the blocks, and restrained only by the brilliant red border of the heart. The first session I had with Alfre, she wished me luck, admitting that she doesn't even sew on buttons. But my job was easy because, as with some of the other quilters, you never really see Alfre working on her block.

Whenever you see close-up hand quilting you are not looking at the hands of the actors, but of actual quilters. Knowing that these scenes would have to look authentic,

Lois Smith as Sophia stitching Finn's bridal quilt.

Lois Smith . . . practiced her stitching technique religiously . . .

I brought in several friends to do the actual quilting. The studio took photographs of the hands of all the actors from the friendship group. I took them to my next guild meeting to try to match their hands as closely as possible to actual quilters' hands. Mainly the likeness just had to be shape and form because, when the quilters got to the studio, they had their hands made-up to resemble even more closely the hands of the actor. They then put on the jewelry and costume the actor wore, especially if the costume had sleeves.

In the scene in the early part of the movie where Finn, as a young girl (see photo on page 37), is sitting under the frame, the feet in costume you see actually belong to quilters as well, Louise Berkley and me. Louise also has the honor of having her hand in the opening credits, making a long stitch.

Alfre Woodard as Marianna quilting *Where Love Resides*.

Some of the stunt quilters in action.

Susan Henry was another hand double who spent a very long, very dirty day at the studio for about twenty seconds of film fame. The day she was there, we were filming part of the wind scene inside on the sound stage and, as I recall, it was cold and raining outside. The special effects crew had two huge fans blow leaves around (as well as anything else that was not tied down) inside a cavernous shell of a building where they had partially rebuilt the house from Santa Paula.

◆

Whenever you see close-up hand quilting you are not looking at the hands of the actors, but of actual quilters.

Another lesson I learned was that making movies is not as glamorous as I thought. It's hard work, very long hours (our call was usually 6 a.m. and we wouldn't leave before midnight), and sometimes under horrible conditions. The filming began in October 1994 and finished in March 1995. The movie was released October 6, 1995. The quilters involved in this project all have a much greater appreciation for the movies we see at the local theater, now that we know how much work goes into getting it on the screen. But we all got to be temporary members of the Screen Actors Guild.

Jan Barbieri, who made *The Grasse Quilting Bee Quilt*, worked as a hand double for two days. Any time you see close-up shots of Ellen Burstyn's hands, you are actually seeing Jan's hands, (except for one scene). Jan filmed the scene where Hy comes in to turn off the desk lamp once Finn has fallen asleep after finishing her thesis. Ellen Burstyn walks into the room, pats the thesis which is neatly piled on the desk and turns out the light. Those are Jan's hands—and she did it perfectly!

Any time you see close-up shots of Ellen Burstyn's hands, you are actually seeing Jan's hands, (except for one scene).

Jan Barbieri hand doubling for Ellen Burstyn.

The next day, while we were watching the film shot the day before, someone noticed that in the title of the thesis a word was misspelled. We had to reshoot the scene and this time, because Jan wasn't there, they used my hands. I was a stand-in for Jan who was a stand-in for Ellen Burstyn. When you see the movie, this scene is so quick you can't read anything printed on the title page, but did you notice the hands?

I felt I owed Kelly Gallagher-Abbott something for the hard work she did at the last minute to complete the label for *Where Love Resides*, so I invited her to come to the studio to act as a stunt quilter. I told her how much fun it would be and left out the bad parts (early call and long, boring hours, sitting around a cold and dirty sound stage). Instead, I emphasized all the good things (Hollywood, bright lights, movie stars, and great food). Besides, her hands were very similar to Lois Smith's.

Ellen Burstyn as Hy

You will notice on *Where Love Resides*, I used a light cream-colored Jeffrey Gutcheon solid fabric for the background. We quilted under very hot lights with make-up on our hands. I was sure the solid fabric was going to be smudged, especially the block Kelly was working on, because it took the most time to shoot that close-up. They used a remote-controlled camera high up and came into an extreme close-up on Kelly's hand quilting. It took several tries to get it just right. To watch the fifteen-second scene in the movie, you wouldn't believe it took ten hours to shoot. But, true to my word, Kelly did get to meet Anne Bancroft, who made a point to come over to meet all the quilters.

As a group I met with the actors four or five times, usually between filming, over in a corner of wherever we were. I wanted them to get comfortable working around a frame, since that would be where most of the quilting scenes would take place. I brought my small portable table frame to the set and put a basted piece of whole cloth in it. It was very informal; whoever was around when the frame was up would come and quilt. If they had to go work, they would leave and then come back later. By this time I wasn't as concerned about their quilting skills, as I was how they interacted sitting at the frame. What happened was totally unplanned—these women became a friendship group. They looked forward to sitting together in this informal

They used a remote-controlled camera high up and came into an extreme close-up on Kelly's hand quilting.

Kelly Gallagher-Abbott preparing for her hand double shot.

Behind the scenes. Clockwise from left: Ellen Burstyn, Patty McCormick, Jocelyn Moorhouse, Dr. Maya Angelou, Lois Smith

setting, away from everything else. They asked me all kinds of questions about my friendship group: what did we talk about? did we eat? (what a silly question for quilters); did we work on individual or group projects? They were just as interested in who we quilters are as a group as we are in them as actors. They have the utmost respect for the work we do and were in awe of each of the quilts I brought to the set. Dr. Maya Angelou would hum or sing to us as we sat at the frame. One evening we got to laughing so hard telling jokes, we were sternly reprimanded and advised to settle down. We talked about holiday plans and our families. One day I told them they were acting just like my friendship group that I had been with the night before. They took that as a compliment.

◆

They were just as interested in who we quilters are as a group as we are in them as actors.

THE FAIRY TALE ENDING

Every story should have a fairy tale ending. The movie premiered in Los Angeles in October 1995. Weeks before that I started campaigning to make sure I would get invited. The same question came up as when I had my first meeting with Amblin: What do I wear to a Hollywood premiere? Christine Dabbs, my crazy-quilting friend, came through for me. She made an exquisite knee-length crazy-patch vest of all black fabrics, each seam stitched with silk threads and beaded. It was stunning. OK, it still looked like I was a quilter, but it didn't look like I was a country cousin.

It was a Wednesday night, so my husband and I had to leave our house around 4:30 to get to Los Angeles on time. I walked out of my house and looked for the limousine, thinking maybe I finally had found the glamorous part of movie-making. No limousine: in fact, my husband had not even washed our car, so now I'm driving in a dirty Jeep to a Hollywood premiere of "my movie." I'm surprised I'm nervous. As usual, the traffic is awful. But we're not late. We park our dirty Jeep ourselves in a parking lot across the street and walk to the theater.

The photographers think I must be somebody and all the flashes start going off.

And then the magic started. There are big movie lights dancing across the sky and the marquee announces the world premiere of *How to Make an American Quilt*. There is a red carpet leading into the theater, and on both sides there are at least fifty or sixty photographers. Now keep in mind this is Los Angeles: any time a crowd gathers, people show up with cameras, not knowing what is going on; but just in case something is happening, they are prepared.

There is someone choreographing the walk down the carpet, so each person gets their moment on the carpet. Our turn comes and, as we step onto the carpet, I realize I am really nervous. All these photographers are looking at me, wondering who I am. I looked great, but not recognizable. Halfway down the carpet, a representative from Amblin Entertainment, Jerry Schmitz, comes out to greet me and I get the Hollywood kiss on both cheeks. The photographers think I must be somebody and all the flashes start going off. What they didn't know was that Jerry was just handing me my tickets to get in to see the movie. By now I'm laughing.

This was the first time I was going to see the movie with the general public. I had seen it twice already, once in a private screening but without the music sound track, and then the night before with the cast and crew at Paramount Studios. There were some

From left to right: Michelle Hilsabeck, Linda Sawrey, Christine Dabbs, Arnette Jasperson, Jane Coscarelli, Kelly Gallagher-Abbott, Patty McCormick

introductions, and Sarah Pillsbury, one of our producers, was kind enough to introduce me along with the director, the actors who were present, and studio executives. It was like being in a movie, being acknowledged from the stage.

Watching the movie, I was more aware of the audience than I was of the movie. They laughed where they were supposed to, and there was a lot of sniffling going on at the end. When we left the theater everyone was quiet, but I was assured by those who knew that it was a good sign.

In the lobby of the theater they had set up a party and hung the quilts. I felt like a princess: so many people wanted to meet me, and non-quilters all wanted to share stories about quilts in their lives or their grandmothers who quilted. It was a wonderful evening and I didn't want it to end. When they were turning out the lights, just about everyone had gone and I was helping take down the quilts when someone came up to me and said I didn't have to do that. You can't take the guild member out of me.

The next night, the studio premiered the movie in Redlands, California (the town we had used to shoot scenes of the individual homes) as a fundraiser for the University of Redlands. My sister Susan, who lives in Redlands, had worked hard to make this happen, along with the women from the University Town and Gown Guild and Jay Brand of Sterling Cinemas.

Whitney Otto, the author of the book, and Murray Miller, the location manager who had chosen Redlands and managed to keep everything together while we worked there, were also invited. There was a reception at the University where each of us spoke briefly about our experience with the movie and then we were whisked to the theater in, finally, a limousine.

Redlands threw a party that rivaled the Hollywood premiere. Two theaters were filled with a lot of my family and friends, as well as two of the quilters who had worked on the movie. Once again I was nervous. Would they like it? What would the quilters think? Needless to say, it got rave reviews.

> *. . . I speak for all of us when I say we are proud of the work we did . . . and of the representation of quilters and quilts in this movie.*

The next night I was in Northern California at the Pacific International Quilt Festival. The quilts were hanging in a special exhibit, and Whitney and I were speaking. Most of the stunt quilters were attending the quilt show, and we went to see the movie as a group the night it opened. In fact, at that 7:00 p.m. showing the majority of the audience was quilters. At one point, sitting next to Kelly Gallagher-Abbott, I asked who was crying behind us and turned around to find out that they all were. It was the scene where the quilt is laid out on the floor and the stunt quilters all got to see their work on the big screen.

I had one more surprise for them, and made them wait to watch the credits. The studio had not intended to include names of the quilters. I learned credits are very expensive and that, as a union movie, they were obligated to list everyone who belonged to a union, which included twenty-two drivers. We didn't belong to a union, but I wasn't going to give in. I felt that listing all the quilters would add credibility to the quilts and to the movie, especially within the quilting community.

These quilts had been made specifically for this movie. And they had been made in the United States, a point important in a movie called *How to Make an American Quilt*. Until I saw the movie the night before the premiere, I didn't know if the quilters would be given screen credit or not. I knew I would be given credit: they had included me between the art and prop departments. I had told them if they included the quilters I wanted to be with them. So we waited, and waited, and then there we were, right between animal trainers and drivers.

It's an odd feeling to see your name in a movie on a big screen, but I think I speak for all of us when I say we are proud of the work we did for this project and of the representation of quilters and quilts in this movie.

The following patterns are from:
WHERE LOVE RESIDES and
MARIANNA'S BABY QUILT

Each block in *Where Love Resides* quilt is a 15-inch finished square. The blocks are divided into quadrants on two or four pages. The patterns for the figures in the Marriage block have not been included here. See sources on page 96 for availability. The corner and a partial repeat of the border are on three pages. Adjust the vine within the border's 12 1/2-inch width around the quilt.

Full-size patterns are included for the six animal blocks from *Marianna's Baby Quilt*. The schematics show how to piece the animals; first into sections, then join the sections to form the block. The borders are then added to complete each block. Measurements are included for each border strip.

Remember to add a 1/4-inch seam allowance to all pattern pieces. Refer to a basic quiltmaking book such as *Quilts, Quilts, and More Quilts!* (C&T Publishing), for additional instructions if needed.

Linda Sawrey's kitten, Lucy, with the original pattern for *Where Love Resides*.

A

Trace and flip for right side of block. Note that the middle flower is not centered in the vase. Make adjustments to stem length of other large flowers.

ALTERNATE BLOCK

C

Trace and flip for right side of block. Note that the middle flower is not centered in the vase.

A

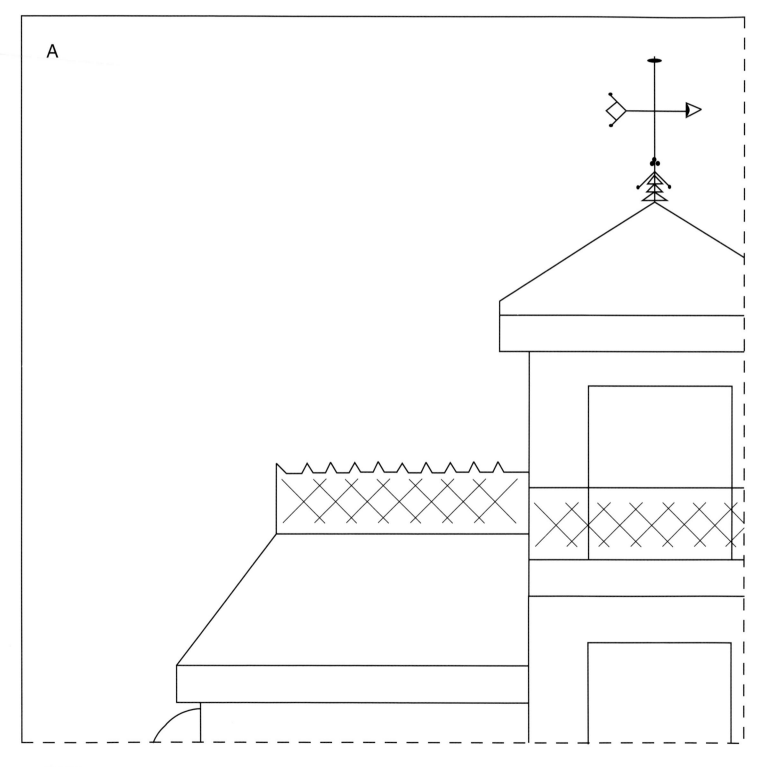

House Block

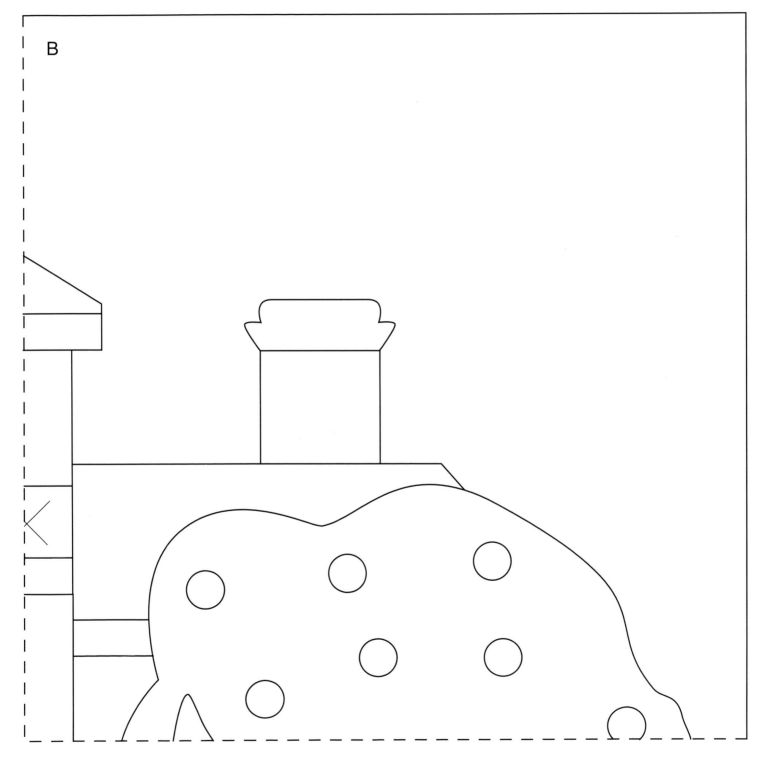

B

C

HOUSE BLOCK

D

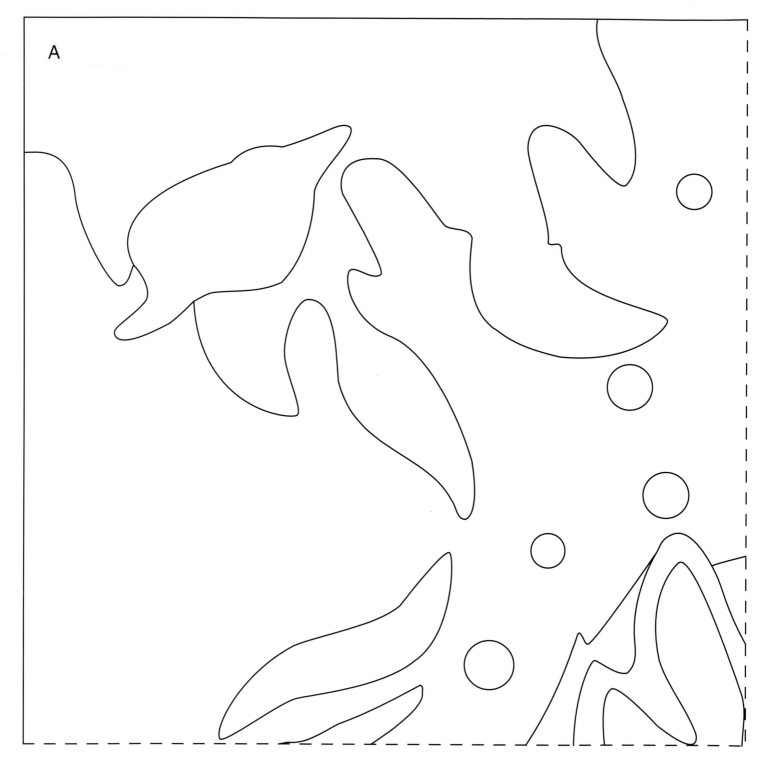

A

Mermaid Block

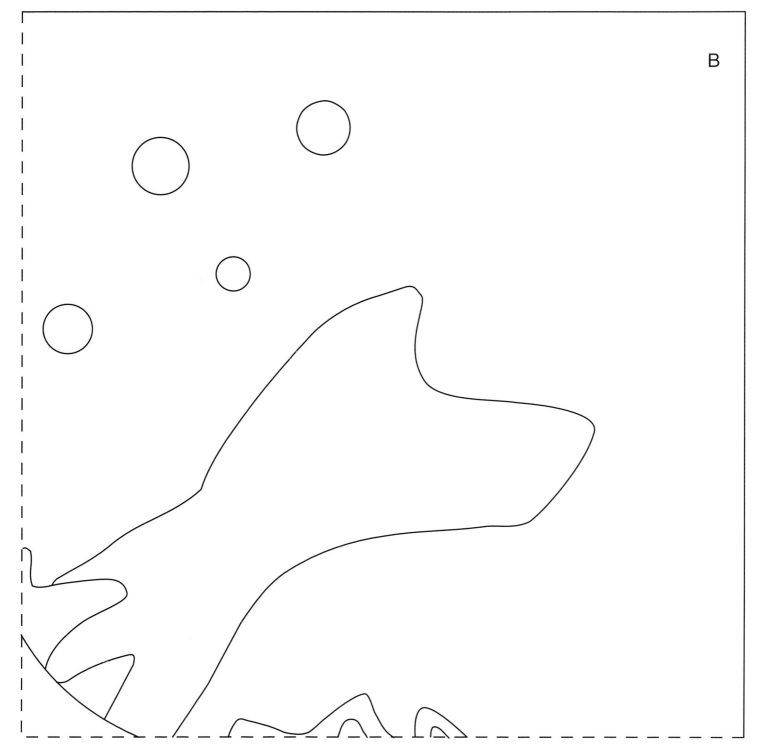

B

C

MERMAID BLOCK

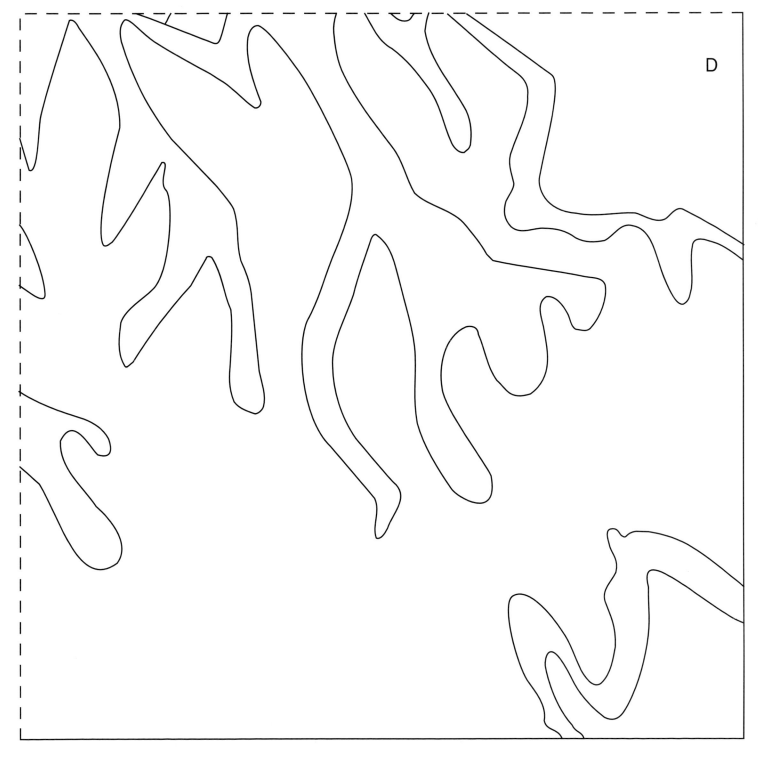

D

A

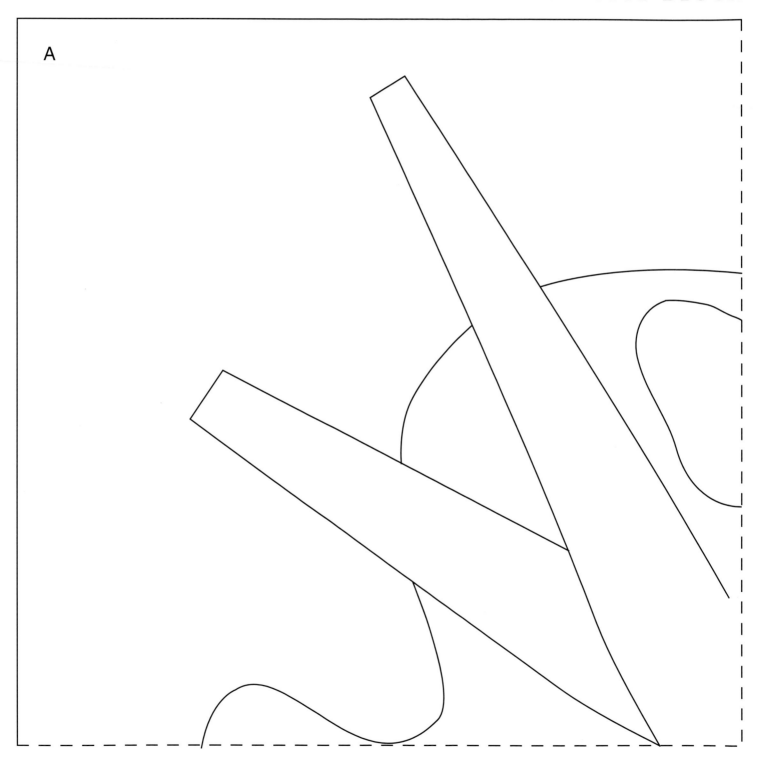

ARTIST'S PALETTE BLOCK

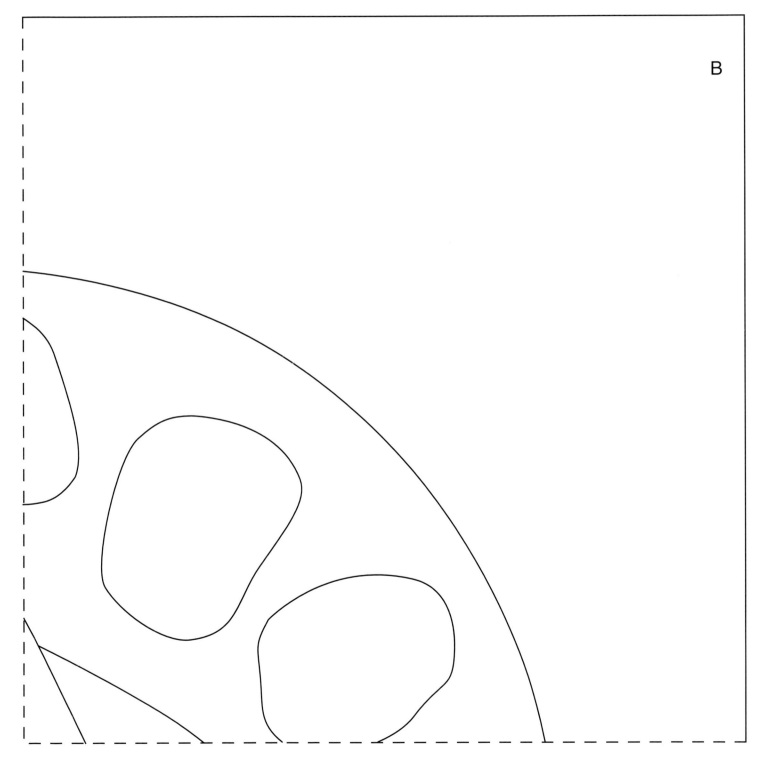

B

C

Artist's Palette Block

D

CRAZY-PATCH HEART BLOCK

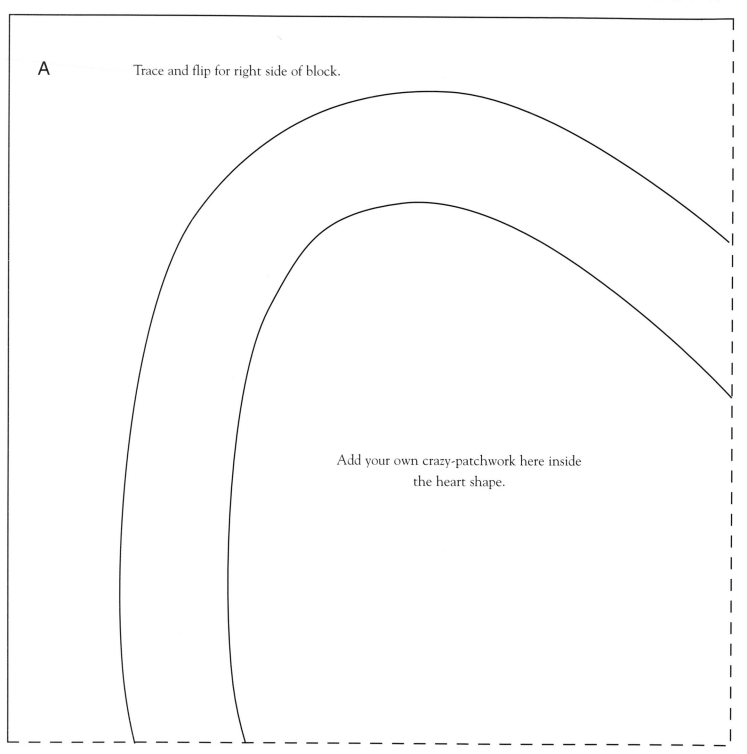

A

Trace and flip for right side of block.

Add your own crazy-patchwork here inside
the heart shape.

CRAZY-PATCH HEART BLOCK

C

Trace and flip for right side of block.

A

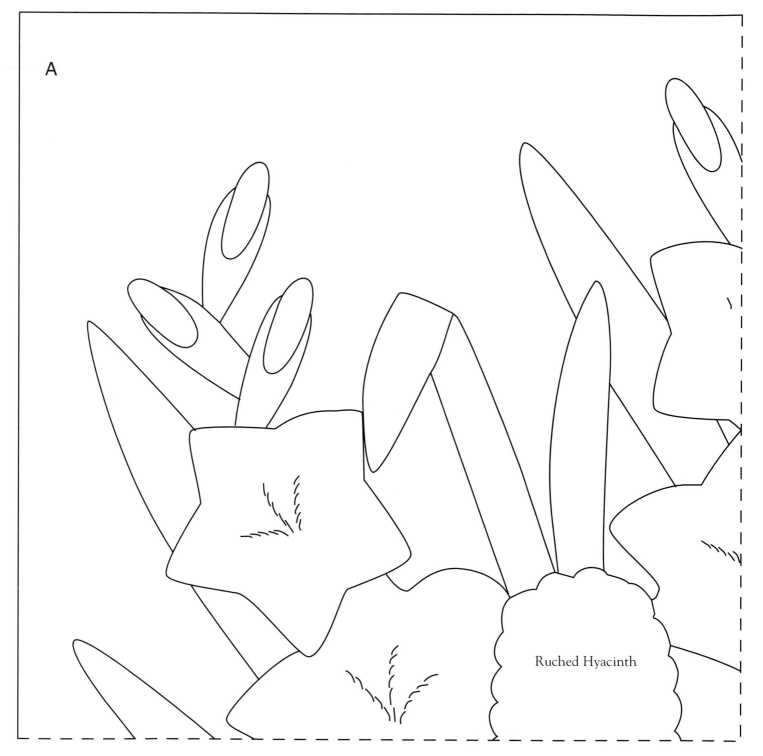

Ruched Hyacinth

GLADIOLI & HYACINTHS BLOCK

B

Ruched Hyacinth

C

Ruched Hyacinth

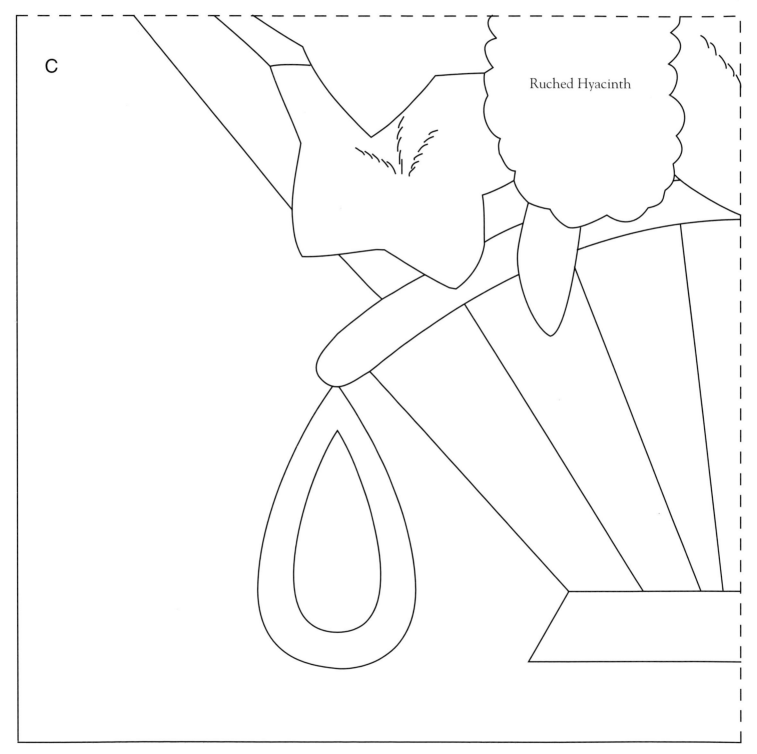

GLADIOLI & HYACINTHS BLOCK

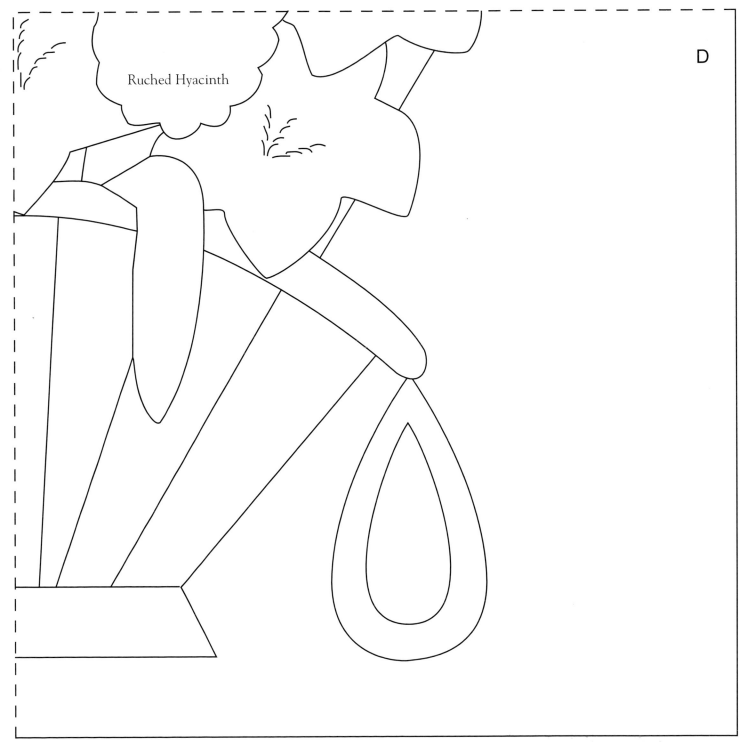

Ruched Hyacinth

D

A

CHICKIE'S GARDEN BLOCK

B

C

CHICKIE'S GARDEN BLOCK

D

B

Trace and flip for left side of block.

RING BLOCK

Trace and flip for left side of block.

Left side of block:
Match dashed lines to extend stem.

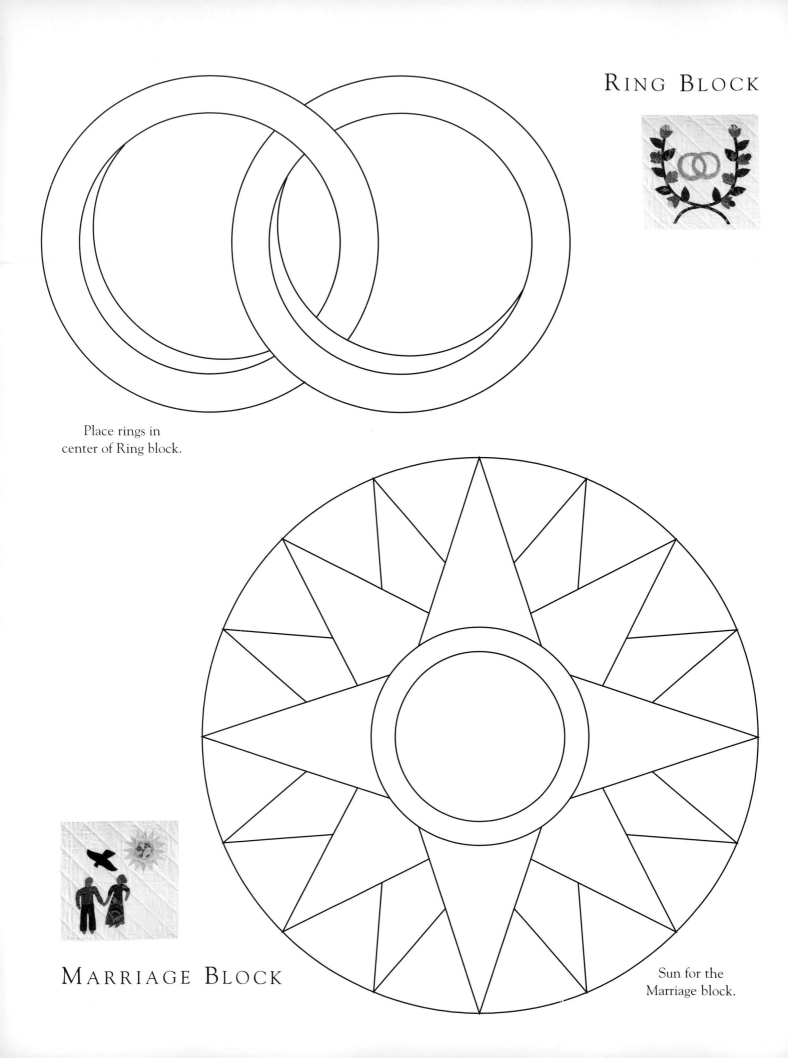

Place rings in
center of Ring block.

MARRIAGE BLOCK

Sun for the
Marriage block.

↟ Extend this line out 1¹/₂″ ↟

↟ Extend this line out 1¹/₂″ ↟

This line bisects the corner.

↑ Extend this line out 1¹/₂″ ↑

↓ Extend this line out 1¹/₄″ ↓

BORDER

↑ Extend this line out 1¹/₂″ ↑

↓ Extend this line out 1¹/₄″ ↓

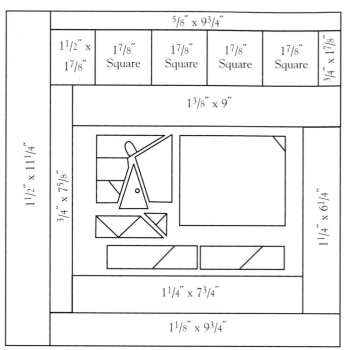

Rhinoceros Block

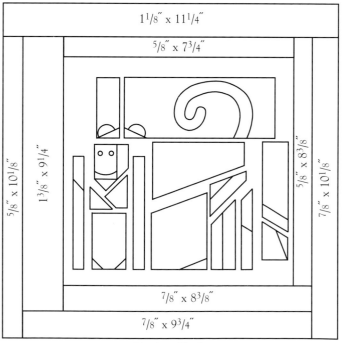

Monkey Block

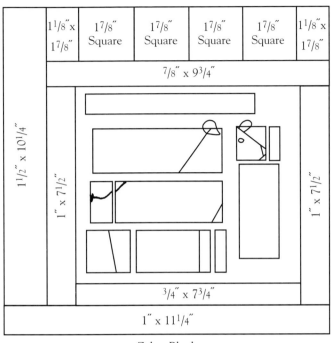

$1^1/8"$ x $1^7/8"$	$1^7/8"$ Square	$1^7/8"$ Square	$1^7/8"$ Square	$1^7/8"$ Square	$1^1/8"$ x $1^7/8"$

$7/8"$ x $9^3/4"$

$1^1/2"$ x $10^1/4"$ · $1"$ x $7^1/2"$ · $1"$ x $7^1/2"$

$3/4"$ x $7^3/4"$

$1"$ x $11^1/4"$

Zebra Block

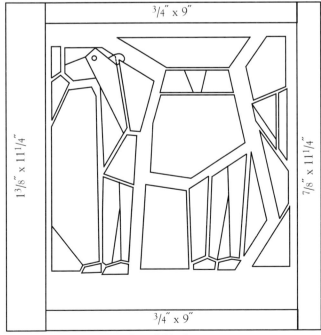

$3/4"$ x $9"$

$1^3/8"$ x $11^1/4"$ · $7/8"$ x $11^1/4"$

$3/4"$ x $9"$

Camel Block

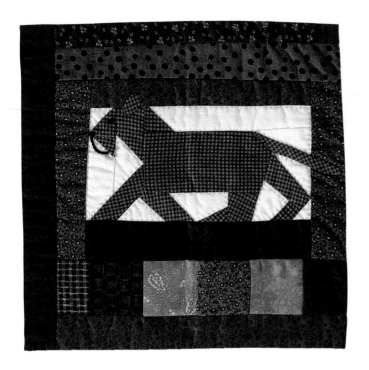

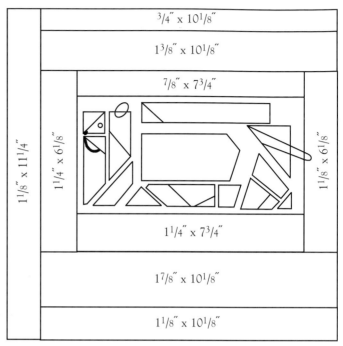

3/4" x 10 1/8"

1 3/8" x 10 1/8"

7/8" x 7 3/4"

1 1/8" x 11 1/4"

1 1/4" x 6 1/8"

1 1/8" x 6 1/8"

1 1/4" x 7 3/4"

1 7/8" x 10 1/8"

1 1/8" x 10 1/8"

Tiger Block

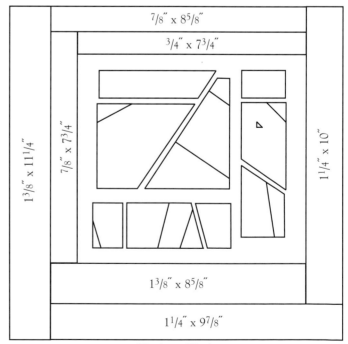

7/8" x 8 5/8"

3/4" x 7 3/4"

1 3/8" x 11 1/4"

7/8" x 7 3/4"

1 1/4" x 10"

1 3/8" x 8 5/8"

1 1/4" x 9 7/8"

Elephant Block

RHINOCEROS

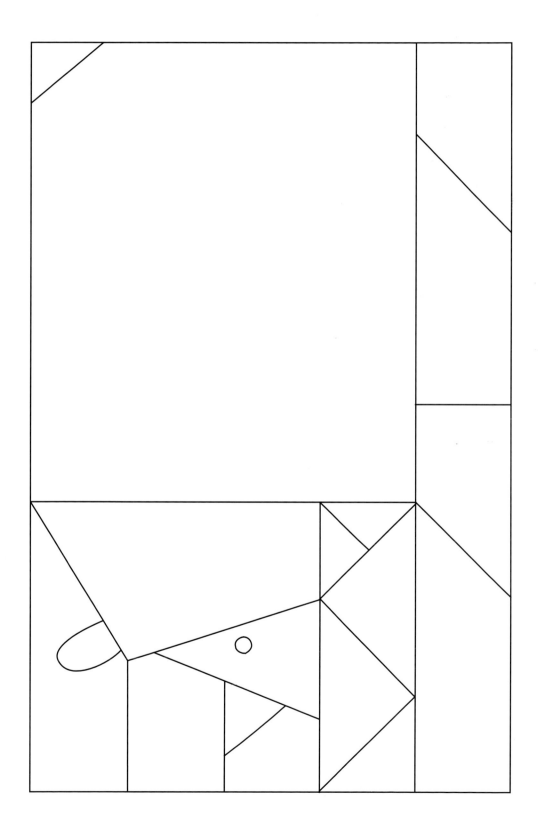

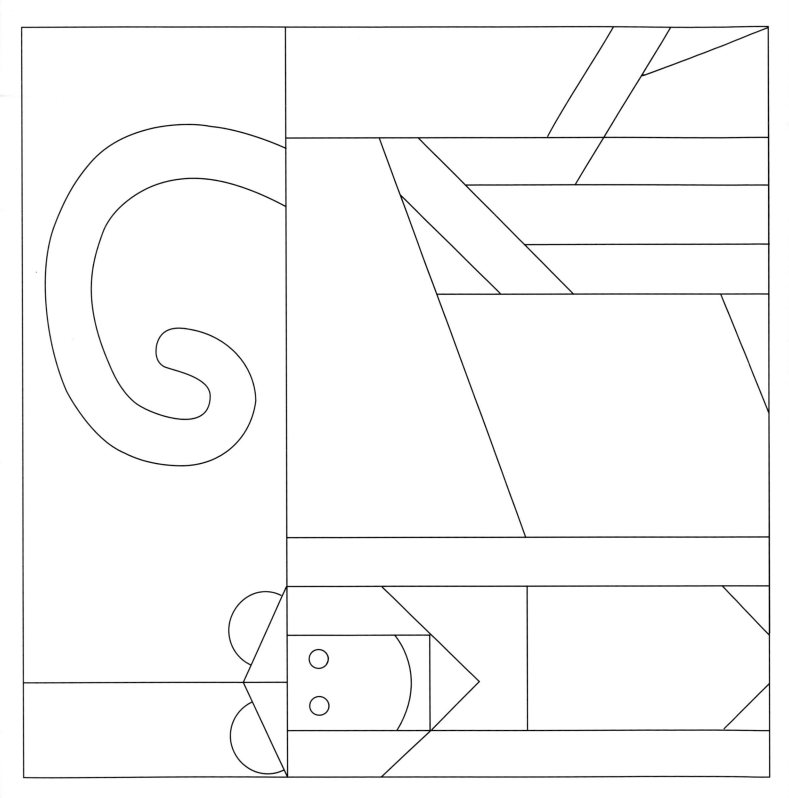

Star & Zebra

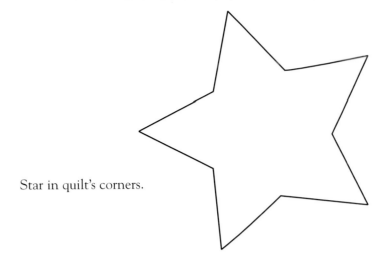

Star in quilt's corners.

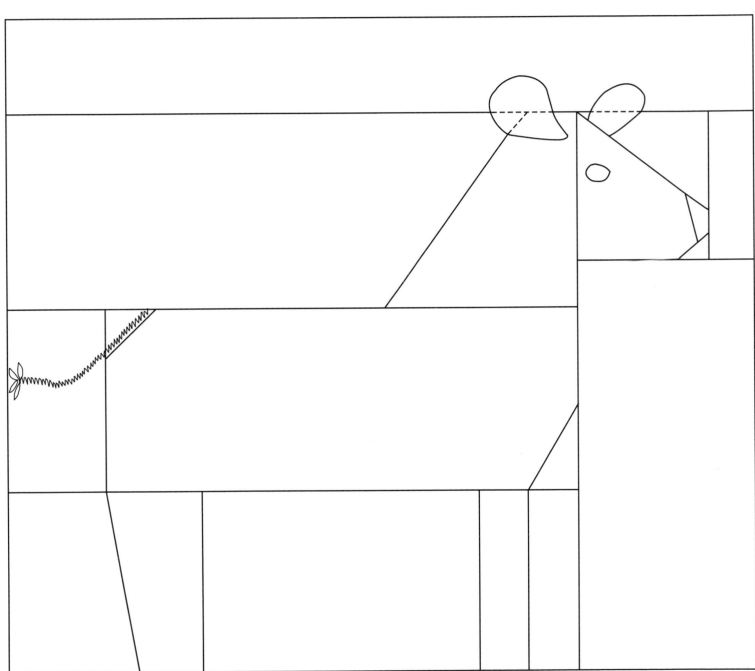

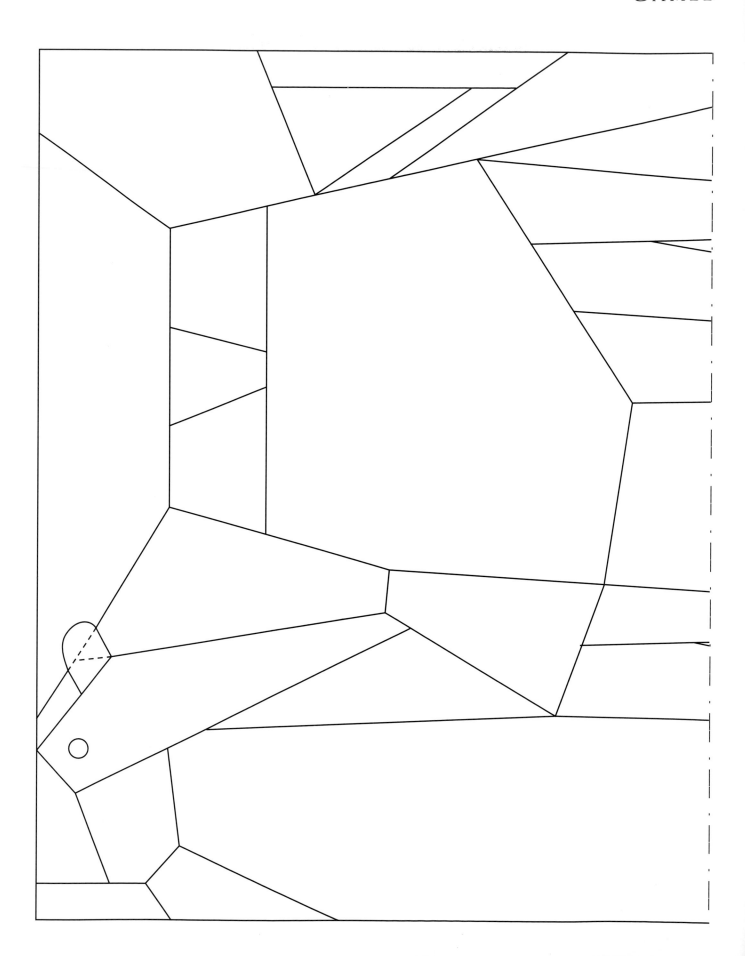

CAMEL & TIGER

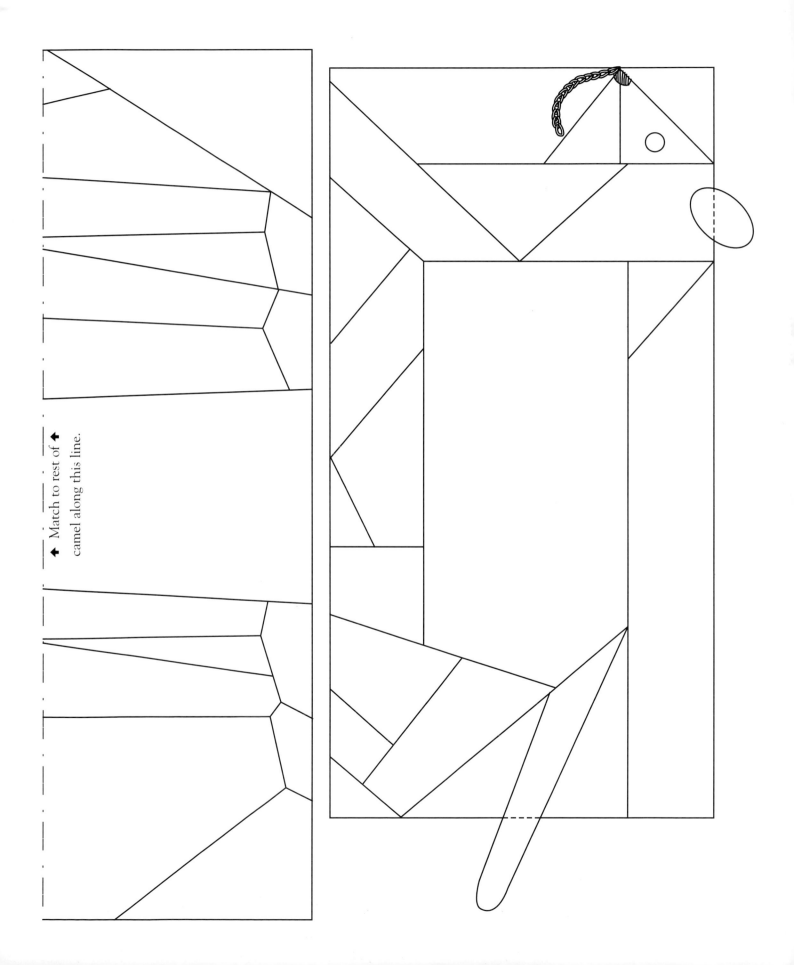

◆ Match to rest of
camel along this line. ◆

Elephant

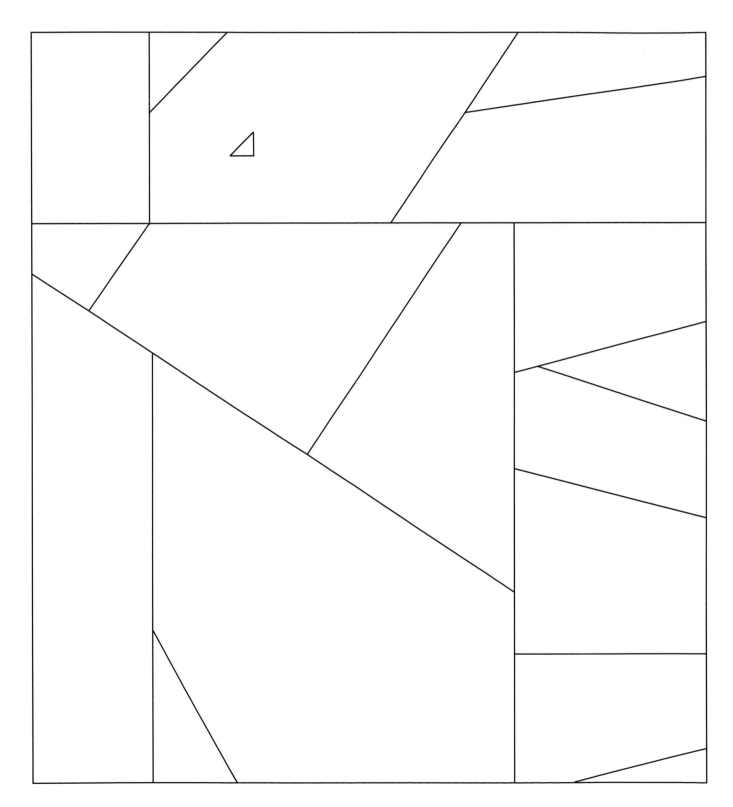

*N*ever realizing where her interest in antiques and quilts would take her, Patty McCormick started quilting fourteen years ago and has since brought her enthusiasm and knowledge to the quilting community and the world at large. She is a founding member of the Flying Geese Quilters of Irvine, California, and of the Valley of the Mist Quilters of Temecula, California. As President of the Southern California council of Quilt Guilds, she was a ready and available resource for the movie industry's query into the art of quiltmaking, a call to which she eagerly responded. Her plans for the next few years include lecturing, traveling, and of course, quilting. Patty and her husband live in Corona del Mar with their two dogs and cat. Watch for Patty's name—her willingness to help and to "make things happen" is sure to lead her to further adventures in the world of quiltmaking.

Patty in one of the director's chairs designed and printed by Cordie Gary. Each cast member had his or her own carefully selected miniature blocks pieced on the back beneath the title.

OTHER FINE BOOKS FROM C&T PUBLISHING:

An Amish Adventure, 2nd Edition, Roberta Horton
Appliqué 12 Easy Ways! Elly Sienkiewicz
The Art of Silk Ribbon Embroidery, Judith Baker Montano
Baltimore Album Quilts, Historic Notes and Antique Patterns, Elly Sienkiewicz
Baltimore Beauties and Beyond (2 Volumes), Elly Sienkiewicz
Beyond the Horizon, Small Landscape Appliqué, Valerie Hearder
Buttonhole Stitch Appliqué, Jean Wells
Christmas Traditions From the Heart, Margaret Peters
Christmas Traditions From the Heart, Volume Two, Margaret Peters
Colors Changing Hue, Yvonne Porcella
Crazy Quilt Handbook, Judith Montano
Crazy Quilt Odyssey, Judith Montano
Dimensional Appliqué—Baskets, Blooms & Baltimore Borders, Elly Sienkiewicz
Elegant Stitches: An Illustrated Stitch Guide & Source Book of Inspiration, Judith Baker Montano
Everything Flowers, Quilts from the Garden, Jean and Valori Wells
The Fabric Makes the Quilt, Roberta Horton
Faces & Places, Images in Appliqué, Charlotte Warr Andersen
Fantastic Figures: Ideas & Techniques Using the New Clays, Susanna Oroyan
Heirloom Machine Quilting, Harriet Hargrave
Impressionist Quilts, Gai Perry
Landscapes & Illusions, Joen Wolfrom
The Magical Effects of Color, Joen Wolfrom
Mariner's Compass: An American Quilt Classic, Judy Mathieson
Mariner's Compass Quilts, New Directions, Judy Mathieson
Mastering Machine Appliqué, Harriet Hargrave
Nancy Crow: Improvisational Quilts, Nancy Crow
Papercuts and Plenty, Vol. III of Baltimore Beauties and Beyond, Elly Sienkiewicz
Pattern Play, Doreen Speckmann
Pieced Clothing Variations, Yvonne Porcella
Patchwork Quilts Made Easy, Jean Wells (co-published with Rodale Press, Inc.)
Quilts for Fabric Lovers, Alex Anderson
Quilts, Quilts, and More Quilts! Diana McClun and Laura Nownes
Schoolhouse Appliqué: Reverse Techniques and More, Charlotte Patera
Small Scale Quiltmaking: Precision, Proportion, and Detail, Sally Collins
Soft-Edge Piecing, Jinny Beyer
Stripes in Quilts, Mary Mashuta
Symmetry: A Design System for Quiltmakers, Ruth B. McDowell
3 Dimensional Design, Katie Pasquini
Tradition with a Twist: Variations on Your Favorite Quilts, Blanche Young and Dalene Young Stone
Trapunto by Machine, Hari Walner
A Treasury of Quilt Labels, Susan McKelvey
The Visual Dance: Creating Spectacular Quilts, Joen Wolfrom

For more information write for a free catalog from:
C&T Publishing
P.O. Box 1456
Lafayette, CA 94549
(1-800-284-1114)

Pattern for the Marriage block from Where Love Resides *available from:*
The Quilt Connection
Barbara Brown
P.O. Box 465
Odenton, MD 21113
410-674-8226

Patterns, supplies to make your own labels, and kits designed by many of the quilters featured in this book available from:
Jukebox
Kelly Gallagher-Abbott
14128 Cameron Lane
Santa Ana, CA 92705
714-731-2563